Beyond the
MIRACLE
Beyond the
GRAVE

A Medium's True Experiences

Melissa Gabriel

BEYOND THE MIRACLE, BEYOND THE GRAVE: A MEDIUM'S TRUE EXPERIENCES

1405 SW 6th Avenue • Ocala, Florida 34471 • Phone 352-622-1825 • Fax 352-622-1875
Website: www.atlantic-pub.com • Email: sales@atlantic-pub.com
SAN Number: 268-1250

Library of Congress Cataloging-in-Publication Data

Names: Gabriel, Melissa (Psychic medium), author.
Title: Beyond the miracle, beyond the grave : a medium's true experiences / Melissa Gabriel.
Description: Ocala : Atlantic Publishing Group, Inc., 2019. | Summary: "True stories the author has experienced as a medium, starting with her miracle healing. Stories include loss of family and friends and what she saw as a medium. Spiritual readings that were validated. Her growth as a medium. Personal stories of love and faith"—Provided by publisher.
Identifiers: LCCN 2019022968 (print) | LCCN 2019022969 (ebook) | ISBN 9781620236505 (paperback) | ISBN 9781620236512 (ebook)
Subjects: LCSH: Gabriel, Melissa (Psychic medium) | Mediums—Biography. | Mental healing. | Spiritual healing.
Classification: LCC BF1283.G23 A3 2019 (print) | LCC BF1283.G23 (ebook) | DDC 133.9/1092 [B]—dc23
LC record available at https://lccn.loc.gov/2019022968
LC ebook record available at https://lccn.loc.gov/2019022969

Printed in the United States

PROJECT MANAGER: Katie Cline
INTERIOR LAYOUT AND JACKET DESIGN: Nicole Sturk

Over the years, we have adopted a number of dogs from rescues and shelters. First there was Bear and after he passed, Ginger and Scout. Now, we have Kira, another rescue. They have brought immense joy and love not just into our lives, but into the lives of all who met them.

We want you to know a portion of the profits of this book will be donated in Bear, Ginger and Scout's memory to local animal shelters, parks, conservation organizations, and other individuals and nonprofit organizations in need of assistance.

– Douglas & Sherri Brown,
President & Vice-President of Atlantic Publishing

Table of Contents

The Miracle

May 25, 2002
Carmel, Maine

"911, what is your emergency?" a female voice answered my call.

"I'm in a lot of pain. I can't drive myself to the hospital," I said, my voice barely above a whisper as I struggled to breathe.

"What is your address?"

"5555 Cook Road in Carmel," I answered.

"I'm sending an ambulance, but I'll stay on the phone with you. I can tell you are having a hard time breathing. I'll wait to hang up after the ambu-lance arrives. Is there anyone you want us to notify?"

My brain was so foggy with pain that it took a few minutes to remember that my husband and kids were camping. I was to meet them later after a wedding. *Where is it they are camping?* I couldn't remember. I, in my hazy thoughts, asked her to notify my friend that I couldn't make it to the wedding. It did seem really important at the time.

"Carmel ambulance is not responding; I'm sending Capital Ambulance, so they will be there as soon as they can from Bangor."

"Okay," I responded.

It was a holiday weekend. *I'm not going to make it. I won't be breathing when they get here.* I was convinced with the amount of pain I was in that this was it. It had occurred to me to call my parents, but I didn't want them to find me dead.

As the ambulance pulled in my driveway about 25 minutes later, I thought that at least if they can't save me, they can help with the pain. The EMTs entered my house through the basement door, calling out to find me. They came through the door into my house. The 911 operator said that she would hang up now that they were there and said she hoped I'd be better soon. They found me on my couch on the living room.

The EMT asked, "What's happening? Where's your pain?"

I told him that I felt like I was in a vice—intense pain all around my middle and radiating up my back. I literally couldn't move. He had to lift my arm to take my vitals. He started an IV and gave me morphine for the pain. They put me in the ambulance and drove me to St. Joseph's Hospital. I remember feeling surprised when I was still alive when we got there. The pain was still intense.

My friend, Jeannette, had heard the call for an ambulance and had rushed to the hospital. She leaned over the railing of the bed, touched me, and said "What's going on?"

I could see the worry in her face. I was so thankful she was there. I told her, "I don't know. I'm in so much pain."

I heard her tell the nurses. They gave me more medicine for my pain—then sweet oblivion.

For about a year previously, I had been trying to develop my mediumship abilities. I had realized that I was more than an empath. I was reading books, doing mediations, and taking classes at a spiritualist camp. I was able to hear my guides and had done a few readings before the events on May 25, 2002.

I had an in-home day care in a finished daylight basement. I loved working with the children. It was the best job I had ever had. A few days previous, one of the kids was sick. The mom called and was desperate—she needed to be at work that day, and he couldn't go to school with a fever. The boy was 10, and it was a low-grade fever. I agreed to keep him upstairs in my house away from the other children. I kept the door to the day care open so I would hear him if he needed anything. Later in the week, he ended up in the emergency room with pain in his legs so bad that he couldn't walk. I found that out later.

By Friday, I was sick. I called the parents and let them know that I wasn't going to take the kids that day. I was rarely sick, so they were all very understanding. I relaxed all day. I had a sore throat, a headache, and body aches. I was the maid of honor in my friend's wedding the next day. I went to the rehearsal and returned home as soon as I could. I lay on the couch, feeling worse. I started vomiting. I was taking acetaminophen for my fever and body aches. I couldn't keep it down, so I took more. I was miserable. I fell asleep on the couch only to awaken moments later to run and vomit again. As it got closer to morning, I was in a deep sleep or so I thought. I felt myself start to come out of my body. I wasn't concerned; I had had out of body experiences as a child and thought that that was what was happening. I coughed and was back in my body. This happened three times. My sleep was so deep. I slept through my friend calling to find out why I wasn't at her house yet for the wedding. I woke up to pain. I realized something was seriously wrong. I tried to get up to go to the hospital and realized that I couldn't even make it across the room. The room was spinning. The pain was getting worse, and I was having a hard time breathing. I reached for the phone and called 911. I checked in with my guides and heard I wasn't going to make it to the hospital. I heard that I was dying. I had always felt like I was going to die young. The pain I was having was very convincing.

As I started to come out of the morphine-induced sleep, I could hear doctors and nurses talking about me. They were trying to figure out what was wrong with me. I couldn't respond. I couldn't open my eyes. I was in and out. I woke up at some point later. The doctor came in and asked if I was taking medicine. I told him acetaminophen. He asked how much. I wasn't sure due to being so foggy and vomiting it up. He had a concerned look on his face as he left my bedside. My parents arrived. My friend had called them. They were still trying to figure out where my husband and kids had gone camping. I fell asleep again.

When I woke up again, I heard the doctor at the foot of my bed talking to my parents. She said, "We need to prepare you. This is probably terminal, she is very sick. Her liver is failing. We don't expect her to survive the next 24 hours. We want to send her to Boston. If there is a liver that becomes available, that is where she would need to be."

My mom started to cry. I felt so sorry that I was going to cause them to grieve.

While preparations for transporting me to Boston were made, one of the nurses hooked me up to an IV of potassium. It burned as it entered my arm. I told the next nurse that it was painful. She turned down the machine pumping into my veins. The first nurse came back and noticed that the machine setting was changed.

She angrily said, "Who changed this machine?" I told her the other nurse had due to the fact it was burning in my arm. She said, "You need to understand this: if we do not get enough potassium in your body, you will not survive the trip to Boston."

They also started me on a medicine to help try to detox my liver of the acetaminophen. This whole time I thought, *I'm surprised I'm still breathing.*

My twin sister arrived to say her goodbyes. I said, "Min, I need you to take care of the girls."

Kayla had just turned 12 the day before, and Joelle was 10. Their dad lived in Kentucky, and I felt that they couldn't lose me and be taken away from all their family and friends that they were close to. They loved their family in Kentucky but never got to spend a lot of time with them at this point.

"Please Mindy, promise me that even if you have to go to court, you'll keep them here in Maine with their friends and family."

Through tears and sobs, she promised that she would. I then felt okay. I could die knowing my babies would have awesome parents in my twin sister and her husband. I knew they would be taken care of and loved. I hugged her, thanked her, and told her that I loved her, not believing I would see her again.

By this point, my husband had arrived. After he had been notified that I was in the hospital, he dropped off my kids with close friends. He and my parents followed the ambulance to Boston.

In the ambulance, I was contemplating my fate. I truly believed that I was dying. I was thinking of the people I was leaving behind. *Will my daughters be okay? Do they know how much I love them? Did I teach them enough to be strong and stay positive? Do my family and friends know how much I love them? Do the ones who made a difference in my life know that they did?* I was wishing that I had said more, expressed my feelings and gratitude more. I was not an overly affectionate or vocal-about-my-feelings kind of person at this point in my life.

I arrived in Boston. They got me admitted to the ICU. I met with Dr. Win Winslow. He was very nice, and I felt like he truly cared. He explained about a possible experimental liver dialysis. There was a team in California that they would fly in to work with me. He was hoping that they would do 10 days of the dialysis, then if they didn't help, hopefully it would keep me alive until I could have a transplant. I continued the medicine to try to detox my liver. It was horrible—the nurse even felt bad when he handed it to me each time. It smelled like old-fashioned hair perm chemicals. I would drink it, and within 20 minutes, I was vomiting. I needed a dose every hour. Then the blood draws started to prepare for the experimental dialysis. Every few hours, a lady came in to draw my blood to monitor my liver enzymes. The woman was nervous about sticking me with a needle and struggled with it each time. One nurse was observing, and after watching her struggle several times to hit a vein, she volunteered to do it for her. I looked at her with gratitude all over my face.

She smiled and whispered, "You have good veins, and I'm not sure what her problem is."

From then on, she followed her into my room and took the blood samples for her. The nurses were amazing and checked on me frequently. I thanked them often for taking such good care of me.

Even though I was receiving excellent care, I was miserable. When my family left me alone for the night, I looked up and thought, *Okay, I'm ready.*

Quite frankly, being a medium, I was very curious about the process, and what it was like. I had always had that strong feeling that I was going to die early, and this was it. I then suddenly felt a warmth like I was lying in the bright sun; it was so warm and comforting. I thought they were preparing me to go "home." Then I was cold and achy and miserable again. By this point, I felt weak and was completely yellow. More detox meds, more blood draws, and more wonderful warmth. When I would feel the warmth, it was as if I was being scooped up and surrounded by love. It was so comforting, even though I felt that it meant that I was getting closer to dying.

In the morning, the nurse came in with a surprised look on her face and said, "Melissa, your numbers are coming back."

I looked at her confused, and she explained that it looked like my liver was beginning to function. That meant more detox, but no more blood draws. I thought that it was because there was improvement, but what I found out later was that they had already denied me as a candidate for the dialysis because I was too far gone. They hadn't expected me to survive this long.

Four days later, I was sent home—no dialysis, no transplant. The doctor was surprised but cautious. He told me not to take vitamins or medicine or drink alcohol for a least a year. I needed to be very careful.

I arrived home and was so happy to see my girls and my step-daughter, Jenna. Friends and family gathered around, and I remember feeling shocked that all these people cared this much.

A couple friends expressed how scared and worried they were. One said through tears, "Melissa, I don't know what I would have done without you."

It occurred to me that I was a much-loved person and that I had been unaware of how much people cared about me.

Four weeks later, I went to Boston for a follow-up with the doctor. They did blood tests. I was feeling fine. I was fully recovered.

I met with the doctor. He looked at me, shook his head, and said, "Melissa, sometimes there are things that happen in the medical field that we have a hard time explaining, but we have a general idea of what happens and how the body works. The liver is an organ that can heal itself, but your liver was dead—not functioning at all—and here you are, sitting in front of me four weeks later, the picture of health. I cannot even begin to explain it."

I felt incredulous when he told me that. I had experienced a miracle.

I do believe the angels healed me so I could continue to do work to help people. It was always my intention with my readings and healings to help people; to help restore their faith or to have faith; to help them know that they are not alone and that their loved ones on the other side do not miss anything. They are here with us when we think about them. WE ARE NEVER ALONE. Even when we think we want to be.

After this event, my mediumship exploded. I saw, heard, felt, and knew more than ever when I connected with the angels or spirits.

Years later, I found out that it was the archangel Gabriel's energy that had healed me. I am, to this day, 17 years past my expiration date and eternally grateful.

Early Years

Etna, Maine

When I was a child, I spent the first five years of my life at Camp Etna, a spiritualist camp that was very popular in the late 1800s and early 1900s during the spiritualist movement. Spiritualists from all over the United States would come to the camp for readings, healings, and classes.

My immediate family were not spiritualists. It was inexpensive housing for a young family. My dad's uncle owned a few of the cottages and his wife was a spiritualist. I have very vivid memories of being a small child in that house that my parents owned—things I should not be able to remember that happened even before I was 2. To this day, I have a vision that feels like a memory of me looking down and seeing my sister and me as infants in our cribs. When I became an adult, I questioned the reality of that by asking my mother, "Mom, when we lived at Camp Etna, were our cribs perpendicular to each other like this?" I demonstrated with my hands.

She looked at me and said with a smile, "Yes, I put them like that because you two would talk to each other. It was like you had your own language."

There were so many memories of really early times that most people wouldn't remember.

When I was 5, we moved to a house that my dad built just about a mile away. My mom was pregnant with my little brother, and, having an older brother and a twin, we had outgrown the cottage at Camp Etna.

I have early memories of not being able to fall asleep at night. It would seem like I would lay there for hours, my sister having fallen almost immediately asleep. I have always moved around a lot in my sleep, destroying my bed. My covers ended up all twisted and sometimes off the bed. My sister across the room never moved. She would get up and pull the corner of her bedspread up, and the bed would look like it hadn't been slept in at all. I would have to completely remake the bed.

I distinctly remember being about 5 years old and laying on my belly and lifting up the back of my jammies because I felt a warm tingle as if someone were rubbing my back. There was no one physically there, but when you're a little kid, you accept weird things without question. Whatever or whoever it was calmed me and I fell asleep.

Before we (it's always a 'we' when you are a twin) started school, I was painfully shy, but my sister was not. I can remember hiding behind my parents' legs when they would talk to someone I didn't know. I remember how they would want me to say my name, and it was painful to have to speak out loud. I have memories of being absolutely terrified of one of my mom's cousins, but have no idea why now.

Things changed when we went to school. I think I felt that she was nervous and I was the big sister (by 18 minutes), and I had to make it easier for her. My mom tells the story of the first parent-teacher conference at the school.

My mom would say, "I asked the teacher how Melissa was doing and told her I worried about her because she was so shy." She went on to say, "the teacher said, 'You mean Mindy, right?'" Mom continued her story: "I said, 'no, Melissa is the shy one,' and the teacher said, 'no, Mindy is the shy one—we can't get Melissa to stop talking.'"

Because I understand energies now, I believe I was sensitive and was easily overwhelmed. That is what created the shyness. I met a little girl a few years ago who was like that, and it helped me to understand my own shyness at that age. She is in a story later in this book.

I had a few out-of-body experiences between 5 and 7 years of age. I can remember after falling asleep, waking up, and looking down and seeing my sister and me sleeping in our beds. Then, feeling cold on my back, I realized it was the ceiling. Then, instantly, I was awake, feeling as if I had been dropped back in my bed.

Apparently, I never said anything to my parents. I wonder if I can partly attribute that to not ever being a morning person. Maybe I wasn't really getting quality sleep while I was out of my body on the ceiling. I was also cursed to live in a household where everyone else was a morning person. I still remember the torturously loud 'good morning's and 'time to get up's! I'd put a pillow on my head and mumble, "I have 5 more minutes." I have always loved my sister, but I did not like her at all before 8 a.m.

Then, eyes half-closed, I'd make my way to the kitchen table for breakfast—noise and happiness all around me and me not liking any of them. They would talk to me and actually expect a response. On the rare occasion I did speak, my dad would say, "Holy cow! Mark it on the calendar, Melissa spoke before she had her cereal." They were amused. I was not.

Being twins, my sister and I had a strong connection. The weird things you hear about twins sometimes happened to us. Sometimes she would complain of a bellyache and I'd be the one to vomit. Or as we got older, I would know that something was wrong with her even if I wasn't with her. I would feel as if something was wrong and wouldn't be able to get her off my mind.

I would call and say, "Okay, what is the matter with you? What is going on?"

She would say, "How do you always know?"

I always attributed it to being a twin.

I realized when I started to date my first husband (the father to my kids) that it was happening with him as well. He wouldn't act upset or say anything or have a look that expressed that he was upset, but I felt it just as physically as if it were my own pain. It didn't happen often, but when it did, I knew it was strange that I was feeling their emotions as if they were mine.

As I got older, I found myself giving advice to friends. When the conversations were finished, I would think, *I'm so clever—I didn't even know that was going on with them.* I would know things without knowing how I knew them, whether in a casual conversation or just randomly.

For instance, we were in my parents' car one day and a song came on the radio. My mom said, "I wonder who sings this song, I like it." A name popped into my head, and I said it out loud. Sure enough, I was right. It was country music. I didn't listen to country and really didn't know many artists. Again, I just thought I was clever.

The Beginning

It had been a busy day with my day care. I love all the kids, but some days it was a relief to see the last of them picked up for the evening. As I headed into the kitchen to make dinner for my family, the phone rang.

I answered, "Hello?"

My friend Nan was on the line. She and I were becoming very close friends. Her husband, Randy, worked with my husband, Matt. We had been getting together socially for a few months.

"Melissa, want to go get a reading from a medium?"

I smiled, feeling excited at the thought. Nan and I had had a few discussions about horoscopes and supernatural-type things; we both found it fascinating. Since I had had some unusual experiences, I was very open-minded.

"Yes—when, where, and how much?" I said excitedly.

As she gave me the details, I felt a sense of anticipation. Not only would it get me out for a night (having a day care in my house sometimes made me feel like I was always home, and I loved getting out of it even for a few hours), but also I was interested to see what would happen. We made our plans to go the next night.

It was a gallery-style reading at a local metaphysical bookstore called Silo 7. The medium was local and had a good reputation. We arrived about 15 minutes before the start of the session. As I browsed the store, I picked up a book. It was about psychic development for beginners. As I read the back cover, it talked about how to manifest things in your life and how to become more intuitive.

I turned to Nan and said, "This would be an interesting read."

Just then, the bookstore owner announced that they were ready to begin. With anticipation, I put the book back on the shelf and took a seat. When the medium got to me, he said that he had my great-grandmother—she was bringing me lilacs. He gave me a few other messages that I thought could apply to me. He hit some people right on with very specific messages. I enjoyed it. As Nan and I left the store, I picked up one of their flyers about other events. On the ride home, we chatted about our experience and decided that we should go again the next time he was there. I thanked her for inviting me and driving.

As I got out of the car and headed into the house, I sighed, wondering what was waiting for me. My marriage was rocky. I was married to a man with anger issues. We had gone to counseling, and he was continuing with anger management classes. His anger was so unpredictable. A lot of the time, I didn't even know why he was mad or what had triggered it. He did have his moments of being kind and loving.

I used to say even to him, "Matt is either the perfect husband or the perfect asshole, and there was no in between."

He had always made fun of anything paranormal, but really I think it just freaked him out. He was not one to watch scary movies. When I came back into the house, surprisingly he was fine. I think he was glad I was spending time with Nan; he liked her.

The next month was December. It was always a busy time of year, and the reading with the medium had made its way to the back of my mind. Family birthdays and Christmas shopping kept me very busy. It was great getting out of the house more often.

Together, my husband and I had three girls; two were mine from a previous marriage. Kayla was 10 and Joelle turned 9 two days before Christmas. Jenna, his daughter from his first marriage, was turning 9 in February. I loved Jenna as if she were my own. The girls were close. My girls lived with us. Their father lived in Kentucky. Jenna was with us most weekends but lived with her mom and step-dad. Christmas sometimes was a challenge to try to see all the families while we had all three girls with us. At this point, we had been together for six years and to not have one of the girls with us when we went to my family gatherings was disappointing.

After Christmas, we got together with some friends. Nan and Randy came to our party. Nan pulled me aside and handed me a gift. I didn't expect it and smiled thinking, *How thoughtful and sweet is she?* I opened it up and found the book on psychic development that I had picked up at the bookstore the night of the reading. I was excited, and I gave her a hug and thanked her. I couldn't wait to start reading it. I loved to read and was very interested in what I would learn from this book. But for now, I set the book aside and went about my hostess duties.

The next day, after cleaning up, I picked up the book, made myself com-fortable, and started reading. I was very interested in learning more about how to develop my intuition. As I read the book, there were meditations to practice. I would put the book down and focus. Random thoughts kept running through my mind, and I thought, *it is impossible to "quiet" my mind.* But as the days and weeks went by, I continued to practice the med-itations and exercises in the book.

Nan and I went back to the bookstore. I bought a pendulum kit. It was a pendulum along with and instruction book. I was excited to get it home and try it out. I wanted to know things. I wanted to ask questions and get answers. I practiced with the pendulum and found that, a lot of the time, it was right. I would even use it to help me find things that I had misplaced.

I really started doing more reading and research on mediumship and psychic abilities. The more I researched, practiced meditation, and used my pendulum, the more I wanted to know. It seemed so right to be learning about this. It gave me something positive to focus on as my marriage was struggling.

I started noticing strange happenings. It was as if the universe was telling me to continue in the direction I was going. One morning, I woke up to the overwhelming smell of sugar cookies baking. It was 5 a.m. and no one was awake and certainly not baking cookies in my house. Later I came to learn that this is called "clairscent" or clear smelling. It is the ability to smell odors through the psychic senses.

Later that morning, I was wondering if I was the only one who had smelled it. It was such a strong scent.

"Matt, did you happen to smell cookies this morning?" Part of me wanted him to say that he had and know there was a logical explanation, but the other part of me didn't want a logical explanation—I wanted it to be physic phenomenon. I wanted to believe that the meditations I was doing were opening me up to be more sensitive.

He just looked at me with a confused look and said, "What are you talking about?"

I explained waking up and the strong smell. "It was like there was a tray of cookies right out of the oven under my nose," I told him. I smiled, thinking it was a warm, comforting type of experience.

He said, "No, it was probably a dream."

I let it go.

As the days went by, I noticed more unusual things. I felt a presence in my car. As I got in one day to run errands, I felt like there was an old lady in my passenger seat. It was like a quick image in my mind, but I could feel something there. It was a quick flash that I thought was my imagination. However, it happened a few times. I started to talk to her. I asked who she was and told her that she was welcome to be my co-pilot, feeling very silly after I said that out loud.

One night, there was this flash of white light in the corner of my bedroom so bright that I was sure Matt would have seen it.

"Did you see that?" I asked, excited.

"What?" he said, giving me a wary look.

I said, "There is something in that corner. It was a bright flash of light. I think something is here."

He looked at me and said angrily, "There is nothing over there." I could tell he was freaked out, but I was excited. For some reason, I had no fear of this.

I naively thought that if it is a spirit, it comes from heaven and is good.

The next day, I sat alone in my kitchen and got out my pendulum. I had been using it with good results. It seemed to give me right answers to 'yes' or 'no' questions. Questions I would ask would be about things coming in the near future, either that day or later, so I would know if I was getting accurate information from the feelings I was getting. I had started to "know" things were going to happen.

That morning, I asked about what had happened the night before: "Did I see a white light in the corner of my room last night?" It swung in a big circle—my 'yes' sign. 'No' was side to side.

"Was it a spirit?" Again a 'yes.'

"Did anyone else see it?" My sign for 'no.'

"Was Matt freaked out?" My sign for 'yes.'

I giggled to myself. I don't know why that was so funny to me—maybe because my husband was 6 feet, 1 inch and 250 pounds and it seemed silly that my 5 foot, 7 inch and 140 pound self wasn't. But it was like that in my household. If there was a strange noise in the night, I was the one who went to investigate. It drove me crazy that when my husband went off on fishing trips and it was just the girls and me in our house, my youngest, Jo-elle, would have nightmares and be scared because he was gone. She always had a fear that someone would break in. I used to tell her that if anyone ever came into our house, it wouldn't be Matt they should be afraid of, it would be the momma bear coming out in me if I ever felt that something was going to harm my babies. This, however, didn't comfort her. If she only knew about the nights I was out with friends and would come home to every light in the house on—even in the bedroom while he slept. It was much later when he told me about a scary paranormal event that made him that way and why he was freaked out by the things I was telling him were happening.

I started talking to other friends about my experiences. There were only a few who were interested and wanted to learn more. My friends Donna and Ginny along with Nan were the people I trusted and asked to join me when I went to the bookstore Silo 7 where we had our readings. I went to the bookstore several times with these women. I usually picked up more books, but one day I bought a John Edward development cassette tape collection. It had caught my eye on previous trips to the store, but I hadn't justified spending the money on it yet although I felt like I had been getting signs. When I would be flipping through the channels to find something age-appropriate for my day care kids, I would come across his show, "Crossing Over." I would get this tingling sensation in my belly every time I stopped on his show; it made me want to pay attention to it. Once I realized what it was about, I would look for the show when I wasn't working. I love John Edward. I couldn't wait to listen to his development tapes.

Things continued to go downhill with my marriage. The bouts of anger seemed to be more happening more frequently. One morning, he came into the kitchen yelling and swearing at me. He called me names and accused me of cheating. That is where every angry outburst ended—with accusing me of having a boyfriend. I had never and would never cheat. One time, during one of the temper tantrums, I was driving in my car, he was in the passenger seat and I had enough. I was feeling like I was going to explode; I was so tired of defending myself and being accused of wrongdoing.

I angrily pulled into a parking lot, slammed the car into park, pointed my finger in his face, and yelled back, "Know this: I don't cheat ever! And I will divorce you before I screw anyone else—any questions?!"

He looked at me, stunned, and it shut him up for the moment. It was rare that I fought back. At least this time we weren't in front of the girls. There were many times that I had to just let him have his fit because arguing back would only prolong it. Most of the time, he would get frustrated with my lack of participation in the argument and how I wouldn't say anything. He would call me a 2-year-old for not talking and eventually leave me alone. I would look at my girls, smiling, and say, "Matt took too many jerk pills this morning—sorry about that." They would giggle, and it would remove the tension in the room.

My family had started to worry about what was going on in my marriage. They had witnessed several unprovoked outbursts. My daughters are very close to my parents and would tell them things about our fights when I wasn't there. I assured them that I was fine. I was so stubborn. I didn't want to admit I had made a bad choice and had another failed marriage.

I found happiness in other things. I loved having my day care. The kids were amazing. I enjoyed every minute of it. The girls loved having me home after I had worked two or three jobs for many years just to make ends meet after their father left. I became good friends with some of the parents—friends still to this day that I don't see often enough. Life gets so busy. Having the day care brought me joy. I could love and have fun with the kids, then send them home at 5 p.m.

During the evenings after I had put the girls to bed, I would listen to my John Edward development tapes. I felt great after doing the meditations and really felt like I was opening up to spiritual energy. One of his lessons talked about doing a white light meditation in the shower. Basically, it told me to see negativity wash off of me and go down the drain, then the water would turn into the white light of God, creating a bubble around me. I started doing it to get rid of negativity that I seemed to absorb a lot of from my husband. At this point, I would feel physical pain in my chest from the stress of it. The meditation was also meant to strengthen my aura to protect me from further negativity.

About two weeks into it—I will never forget—I was standing in my bedroom when Matt came in and started yelling and calling me names again. I thought, *Hmm, interesting.* I was not feeling the stress pain in my chest and I was still in a good mood. It was amazing. This white light meditation really did work. I couldn't believe it. I stood there and listened to his fit and continued to smile, which made him more frustrated. This continued. I did the meditation every day and felt calmer and more peaceful. One day when Matt was being very negative about a friend who was sick and how bad it could get for her, I said, "Maybe it won't go that way; maybe she will get better."

He glared at me and said, "Not everyone lives in Candy Land, Melissa. There is a real world and bad things happen."

I just smiled and said, "I like living here. It's nicer." I really felt that it was true.

I have always been an optimist. I have always believed that things would work out for the best. I remember being upset one time over a breakup with a guy as a teenager. I was crying on my bed, and my mom and grandmother came in to console me. I will never forget one of the things they said. "Everything happens for a reason—if it is meant to be, he will come back."

And my gram said, "And if he doesn't, it's because something better is coming along." It felt so true, and I started to believe it. That had been my thought process for any struggles from then on out. Every breakup and every disappointment was leading me to where I needed to be to be happy. I had an acceptance of this and was able to let things go fairly quickly. I was always the kind of person that, if you make me mad, give me five minutes of listening to some upbeat music and I would be over it. Music has always been my go-to when I'm upset. I think that now I had an understanding and belief that things did happen for a reason, and I believed it was in my best interest to let things go and move on, focusing on the future knowing something better is coming. Again, I am the eternal optimist. Maybe I have always lived in Candy Land.

As I read and researched more, I looked back at my past. I realized that for a long time, I had had a strong intuitive side, remembering the weird things that happened when I was a child.

Tarot Cards

Spring 2001
Carmel, Maine

When I first started going to Silo 7 bookstore, I went often, picking up little things here and there that I thought were cool or that I thought would help me to connect more. One time, I saw a deck of tarot cards and decided to buy them. Silo 7 was offering a course on tarot. It was a couple of nights over a few weeks. The woman who taught the course had written a book on interpreting the tarot cards.

Nan and I took the course. It was fun and we learned a lot. The woman teaching the course was very personable, and I enjoyed her teaching.

I had bought the original Ryder Waite Cards. They are said to be the first and original deck. As I learned more about them from the class and some reading on my own, I developed a very basic understanding of the symbolism. I would do practice readings on myself. I would do the Celtic cross 10-card spread, or sometimes I would do a three-card past, present and future spread. I was amazed at how the cards fell in the positions they did to make the meaning clear for me.

Like I said, I had a basic understanding of the symbolism, but mostly I would get a feeling, or I would read the book that comes with the cards. When I read about the meaning of the card, there would always be a certain part that would stand out to me, almost as if it were in bold print or highlighted. I would "know" that was what I was meant to pay attention to.

I started doing tarot card readings for my friends. I was surprised at how accurate it was becoming. The cards that landed in certain places in the spread gave me an indication of what the question was or what the message was pertaining to. It continued to amaze me. With all the 72 cards in the deck, the fact that they all seemed to land in places that made the reading make sense and give me the direction was building my trust that this wasn't coincidence, these cards were being manipulated by spirit. Friends were impressed. I started to have more confidence in what I was doing.

One night, Erica and Steve came over to visit. Steve was a good friend and ex-boss of Matt, my husband. Erica, his wife, and I were becoming friends. We had spent some time together visiting at their house, and I enjoyed their company. It was a warm night and we were having dinner and drinks outside on the deck. We started talking about my new interest, the tarot and anything of a spiritual or metaphysical nature. I shared some experiences I had. I was saying how it was accurate and I was blown away with what I was getting with the tarot cards. Steve and Matt exchanged a "she's crazy" look and smiled at each other.

Erica was interested. She said, "I would love for you to do a tarot reading for me."

Steve said, "Melissa, I gotta tell you, I think it is all bullshit. I don't believe any of it."

I responded, "Well, I cannot prove it, but how do you explain what has been happening?"

Of course, coincidence or my imagination were the answers the men came up with. Finally, Steve said, "Okay, do a reading for Erica. I'm going to watch."

We went into the house. I felt a little nervous. This was the first time I was going to do a reading in front of an obvious skeptic. I got out the cards, called in my guides, lit a candle, and said a prayer. I had Erica shuffle the cards, and I laid them out in a Celtic Cross Spread. I started to explain about the positions of the cards and what they represented. Then I got into the reading—I was still using the book at times and, again, seeing what I needed to say stand out to me. I would catch Erica and Steve looking at each other. I know they were keeping blank expressions so not to give anything away. At one point, in explaining a card and the relationship to the cards around it, they looked at each other.

Erica exclaimed, "Oh my God, you have to admit that we were just talking about that this morning!" That gave me a little more confidence and I continued.

At the end, Steve said, "Okay, so I can't explain it, but you were very accurate. I'm not sure how this all works, but you definitely have something here."

Erica explained and validated things that I had said during the reading. I can't say that Steve was a believer that night, but I do believe it made him question what he thought was impossible.

Camp Etna

GUIDANCE
Spring 2001
Etna, Maine

Camp Etna is a spiritualist camp. It has been around since the late 1800s. In its heyday, it brought in spiritualists from all over. Thousands of spiritualists would arrive in the summer for various spiritual activities, healings, readings, church services, and teachings. Spiritualists believe in the continuation of life after the change called death. We believe that the communication with the so-called dead is a fact. It is a very open-minded, nonjudgmental religion in which I have found a home. To this day, it still has a wonderful summer program. It brings in mediums from around the world. I had no idea that it was such a special place until I was an adult. Having lived there as a small child, I now credit some of my "sensitivity" to having spent my first five years of life there. It is said that the camp resides on top of ley lines that intersect. Ley lines are said to be lines of positive energy in the earth. Some believe they connect to ancient sacred sites or places of spiritual energies or vortexes.

Thinking about this led me to go to Camp Etna. I remembered talk of a "Healing Rock." I didn't remember what it was like or have any memory of it but wanted to go investigate. I went with my friend Nan. It was a chilly spring day. The sun was out but there was still a coolness to the breeze. We walked a short way on a path in the woods to the healing rock.

"Here it is," I said.

Nan and I looked at each other. It was smaller and deeper in the ground then we had anticipated. We squatted down and placed our hands on the rock. Sure enough, we both felt energy. To me, it felt like a deep, throbbing pulse. I felt my own pulse to make sure I wasn't just feeling it in my hands. No, it was different; it was slower. It was barely there, but there it was.

We sat there for a few minutes before we started to get cold. It was interesting. I hadn't been to Camp Etna since I was a kid. Everything seemed smaller. The cottages seemed tiny. I saw the small, old cottage I had lived in. It had seemed big when I was 5. I remembered more as I looked at an old-fashioned water pump near the house. My older brother would pump water into buckets and take it in his wagon to an elderly woman who didn't have running water. He was probably 6 or 7 at the time. I smiled, remembering playing on the hill in front of the temple. I remember feeling angry when they were doing repairs on the temple that continues to sit in the middle of the campgrounds because we were not allowed to play there during the construction. I smiled to myself, remembering meeting my friend Christine. My sister and I were 4, and she was 3. Her parents had come down to talk to my parents and she followed us in and back out of the house. I remember every detail like it was yesterday. I could almost hear our girly giggles. I felt very nostalgic as we looked around.

As we were headed back to my car, a man approached us. I'm sure it wasn't usual for them to see strangers down there that time of year; summer opening was still a couple months away.

"Can I help you with something?" he said. He was a tall, elderly man with a scraggly beard. Something about him seemed very calm and gentle.

"No, we are all set; we were just leaving. I used to live here when I was a little girl. I'm just bringing my friend to see the healing rock and see the place again," I explained. "I'm Melissa, and this is my friend Nan."

He took my hand that I had extended towards him. He introduced himself as Dewey Grant. An interesting look came over him. "I think you should come meet my wife, Arlene," he said.

Nan and I looked at each other and shrugged. "Okay, sure," I said. I was thinking that maybe they just wanted some company.

We met Arlene. I liked her instantly. She was originally from New York, and you could hear a slight accent. She had white hair but still had a strength about her like she could handle anything that came her way. She was very straightforward. We talked about where I used to live and who I knew. We talked about my great uncle. They didn't remember him, and I didn't remember the people she talked about, being so young when we moved. They lived in the house directly beside the house that I had once lived in. She knew who lived there before and after we did.

We discussed my interest in spiritualism. I talked about some experiences I started having. This is when I found out Arlene is a medium.

"The light is very strong with you. You are a medium. You used to talk to spirits when you were little. I'm getting you stopped when you were living at your grandmother's house. Something scared you upstairs in that house," she said confidently.

I thought, *wow*. She didn't have prior knowledge of my living at my grandparents' house. We stayed with my grandparents for a short time while our house was being built. I did remember feeling scared sometimes upstairs and didn't want to be alone up there. I told her that I didn't remember what scared me.

"You did live in your grandparents' house, though, didn't you?" Again, she knew.

I said, "Yes, and I do remember not liking to be upstairs alone." I was very intrigued.

She said, "You should take classes."

I said, "I will look into finding one."

We chatted more. I told her that I lived in Carmel now and had a home day care. I enjoyed meeting them. I was smiling when Nan and I left. I felt validated. Developing my sensitivity was the right direction for me.

The next day, I looked into classes. I found one. A gentleman named John Flood was teaching a development class in Bangor. I signed up. It was to start in a couple weeks. In the meantime, I played with my divination tools and practiced my meditation. I thought I was hearing my guides during meditations but doubt was in my way.

I took a few classes at the bookstore. One was on connecting with angels. As I listened to the woman teaching the class, she described her experience when she connected with an angel for the first time through meditation. In this class we were to connect with archangel Gabriel. In meditation, I had a similar experience that the woman teaching the class had described. I felt amazed.

Later, on my way home, I questioned, *Did I make that up because that was how she described it?* I asked for a sign. "Did I connect with Gabriel? Please show me a sign," I asked out loud in my car.

I wasn't sure what I would get for a sign, but I told myself to be open to it. A few minutes later, the song "Iris" by the Goo Goo Dolls came on. I thought, *That's it!* That song is from the movie "City of Angels." It wasn't played much anymore. Since it happened a few minutes after I asked, I was excited. A little later, I told myself that is was coincidence. It is amazing how we dismiss so easily yet need so much to convince us.

I got ready for bed, and my logical mind kicked in again. Was it really a sign? I set my alarm and climbed into bed. My alarm is set to a radio station. I enjoy waking up to music and absolutely hate annoying, beeping alarms. When my alarm went off in the morning, the song that was playing made me smile.

I thought, *Okay, I get it,* as I listened to the rest of the song "Iris" by the Goo Goo Dolls. That started my day out on a great note. It couldn't be coincidence to hear that song twice in less than a 12-hour period when it wasn't a current hit.

As I was getting ready for my psychic development class, I received a phone call. John, our instructor, was sick; his wife, Darlene, was going to be teaching the class in his place. She asked if I was okay with that. I said that I would be; I was excited for any guidance.

I went to the class and met a few people. I had a good feeling about the group and the space where we were meeting. I was excited to get some actual training. I think that, deep down, I wanted it confirmed that I was experiencing psychic/medium happenings and I wasn't crazy. We discussed different types of abilities and did some guided meditations. I really enjoyed the class and my fellow students. We were to meet again the next week.

The next week, I received a call that John wasn't feeling well still and that his wife would be teaching the class again. Since I had enjoyed the first class, I was just fine having Darlene instruct me.

I also took another class at the bookstore. This one was on spirit communication. During the beginning of the class, a woman was talking about how she knows she gets signs from her mother who had passed. She talked about receiving cards that have flowers on them that are her mom's favorite.

In my head, sounding like my own thought, I heard, *Tell her I love her, tell her I love her, tell her I love her.* It was repeating quickly over and over again.

I thought, *Why am I thinking this? I don't know her.* Then it struck me that the pronouns were wrong. If I was thinking it, I would be thinking, *Tell her you love her.*

So, I thought, *Who is this?* I believe I heard the name Veronica.

I had never experienced anything like that before. I was not confident enough in what I heard to say anything. I just sat there. I started to feel bad, like I was really disappointing someone. I felt very guilty. It got so uncomfortable that I finally interrupted the woman and said, "I've never done this before. I don't really know what is happening, but in my head, I heard 'tell her I love her' over and over again."

The woman smiled and said, "Oh, thank you, it's my mom!"

I said, "No, it isn't." That part was out of my mouth before I realized I was saying it. How I knew Veronica wasn't her mother, I had no idea. I said, "She said her name was Veronica."

The smile faded a little, but she said, "I don't know a Veronica, but I'll take that with me."

I felt horrible. Not only did I interrupt her, I was wrong.

After the class, the woman approached me to thank me for the message.

"I've never gotten a message like that before," I replied. We chitchatted about some of our thoughts about how spirits communicate with us. I enjoyed our conversation and we exchanged numbers. It was always good to meet someone else who was also open-minded.

A week went by. My phone rang. It was the woman from the class. "Melissa, I just saw a rainbow."

"Oh, nice," I replied, feeling confused as to why she would call to tell me that.

She said, "You don't understand—rainbows make me think of this one person. When my Mom was in the hospital with her long-term illness, there was a woman in the room with her. We became very good friends. Even after my mom passed, I continued to visit her. We played cards and really enjoyed our time together. We were like family. Her name was Veronica! As soon as I saw the rainbow, it dawned on me that is who you were hearing."

I was so excited to hear this; I could have jumped up and down and squealed. I thanked her for calling and told her how much it meant to me.

She said, "No, thank you! It means a lot to hear from her."

I hung up and was so excited! This was real!

Later that week, I was scrolling through TV channels and came across "Crossing Over." As I saw John Edward give a message, I felt this intense sensation in my belly. I listened and heard, *You need to go do a healing for John Flood.*

I thought, *I don't know him.*

And I heard, *You do here.*

I asked, *What do I do?*

I heard, *Go there, and the angels will work with you.*

I was nervous and unsure when I called Darlene on the phone. She was very open to the idea. Knowing me from class, she trusted me. She invited me to the hospital the next day.

As I drove to the hospital, I felt nervous and excited. I wasn't sure what I was doing, but I had this energy flowing through me. I felt excited, and my hands were warm and tingling.

I arrived at the hospital and went up to his room. I walked in, and he was very medicated. Darlene introduced me, but he seemed very unaware. I sat beside the bed and asked if we could roll him over. I put my hands on his back and just visualized white light coming down from above coming through me, into my arms, out my hands, and into John. Then I felt my hands move back as if someone else were moving them and had a vision of them filling with blackness. I felt like I was pulling the sickness out. My hands continued to move on their own. I was feeling lightheaded and calm, like I was in a deep meditation. My hands started to move together slowly then clasp. The blackness had disappeared as my hands moved together like it was evaporating.

I heard, *The choice is up to him now. He will decide to either stay and recover or to cross over.*

I don't remember if I said that to Darlene. I vaguely remember walking to my car and feeling strange and lightheaded as if I had been drinking alcohol. I was excited to have had that experience. At the time, I really did believe that there was an angel moving my hands and pulling sickness out of John through me.

Minutes later, my logical thought processes kicked in, and I questioned what I had just experienced.

"Did an angel really work through me?" I asked. "Please give me a sign."

I was driving and looking for a store on Stillwater Avenue in Bangor. I realized all of a sudden that I had gone past it. I immediately put my blinker on and made a left-hand turn into the first driveway. As I pulled in, I realized that I was turning into a place where "Angel's Hair Care" and "Natural Healing Center" were located in a little business park. I thought instantly that this was my sign. I had driven to that store before and knew where it was but had been distracted, only to pull into a lot where "Angels" and "Healing" were literally on signs. It was very interesting. Of course, I questioned again, but on the drive home, I heard "Iris" by the Goo Goo Dolls.

A few days later, I received the news that John had passed to spirit. Our development class was canceled. I remember thinking after I expressed my sympathy and hung up, *What now?*

I looked up and said, "If this is really the direction I'm supposed to go in, I need help. Please show me where to go from here."

There were no other development type classes anywhere in my area. I was at a loss for what to do next. I went back to reading and meditating. I enjoyed my day care, and my photography business was busy with spring sports photos and weddings. I enjoyed time with the girls. My marriage had its moments, but we were very distant. I took to sleeping in another bed or on the couch. I blamed it mostly on his snoring, but it was just easier.

A few weeks went by. Spring was turning into summer. It was a beautiful sunny day. I had just brought the kids back inside and was getting them settled when there was a knock on the door. I went to the door and looked out the window. I was startled to see Dewey Grant standing there. I hadn't seen him since that day at Camp Etna. I thought, *How did he find me? Is he looking for me?*

I opened the door and said, "Hi, Dewey. Nice to see you."

"I knew I'd find you," he replied. "I had to come tell you that they are starting mediumship development classes at Madison Spiritualist Camp and I needed to come tell you. Arlene and I are going if you want to follow us there. They will be on Wednesday nights at 6:30 p.m. starting next week."

Without hesitation, I agreed to go. "What time should I meet you?"

"Probably by 5 p.m. I'll meet you at the end of the Camp Etna road."

I agreed and thanked him for thinking of me.

He smiled and said, "I'll see you Wednesday."

He left; I looked up and said, "Thank you!" Dewey knew that I lived in Carmel but that was all he knew. He was definitely guided to me. I knew then that I was most certainly supposed to continue on this path. I could hardly wait for Wednesday to get here.

Teachers

Madison Spiritualist Camp was a spiritualist camp similar to Camp Etna. During the summers, there are mediums who visit to teach classes and workshops as well as do private readings. Sunday service is also held each Sunday through the summer in the small temple. Madison Spiritualist Camp is on a lake in Madison, Maine. It is a beautiful peaceful area. Lakewood Theater is close by—a popular attraction that, in its heyday, had some well-known actors.

The Wednesday of mediumship development classes finally arrived. I met Dewey and Arlene and followed them for about 45 minutes before arriving at Madison Spiritualist Camp. I met John Davidson, the Medium leading the class. He was a tall, thin man with white hair and a beard. He had a gentle energy and a welcoming smile. I instantly trusted him.

We all introduced ourselves. I was nervous but so excited to meet others on a similar path. We did a guided mediation and John talked about how the spirit works with us. It was an amazing class, and when we were done for the night, I had a sense of disappointment that the time had flown by so fast. I was hooked; I couldn't wait until the next class.

We continued to meet weekly. Arlene and Dewey didn't attend any other class. I felt that they were the catalyst to get me there. When I was in class, I received more feelings, messages, and guidance from Spirit. I was now hearing Spirit, and it was getting clearer and clearer. John would give us messages that he was receiving to help guide us.

One message he gave me was: "Be careful what you wish for; you are going to have all the senses. You will hear, see, and feel all of it. It will get overwhelming for you if you don't go slowly."

I didn't know if I believed him because I was still so skeptical at this point about what I was hearing or if I just wanted it all. I wanted to be able to help people. I wanted to be able to help people restore their faith and know that they are not alone. What I didn't know at the time was how accurate that was, but that is another story in this book.

During one of my meditations, I heard, *Melissa, do you know who I am?*

I knew it was a female, and it felt so familiar that I just knew who she was.

Freda, I thought.

And I heard, *Yes.* She was my great-aunt.

I was surprised and so happy to hear from someone whom I had loved and respected so much. We didn't see her often when I was growing up. She was my paternal grandfather's sister. At this point, she had passed to Spirit several years ago. She was the one who organized our very large family reunions. She was so loving and quick with a smile and hugs. I remember that, when she would visit my grandfather, all of us kids would be excited. "Aunt Freda is here!" one of us would yell, and we would run to see her. She hadn't realized this. I was sharing my thoughts and emotions about her during this first time connecting.

She became a guide and teacher on the spirit side for me. For a few weeks, there were lots of interactions. We communicated through thoughts in my head and I heard her responses in the same manner. We would work on my "seeing." She would show me in a flash of a vision or image in my mind, and I would describe it to her. She answered my many questions. She was always there when I wanted to "talk."

After a few weeks of working with her several times a day on a daily basis, she passed me on to another guide. This guide was male and again we practiced visions and hearing.

One day, I was standing at the sink doing dishes, and I thought about how I hadn't heard from Aunt Freda in a while. I'd been working with the other guide, but I missed talking to her. No sooner had I thought that, than I heard her.

I was surprised. *What—do you spirits wear a beeper and when we're thinking of you, it goes off?* I joked.

She replied, *No, but that was a good analogy. It is more about the energy of the thought.*

It was more complicated than I was interested to know, so I left it at that. Now I understand—our thoughts are energy and they do connect with our spirit loved ones. Beyond all reasonable doubt, you can know that if you think of someone on the other side, they will hear you and will be there with you.

During my classes with John, he continued to encourage me. One day, he received a message for me. He said, "Melissa, I do not know all about Bible verses, but I'm getting that you should read this—1 Corinthians 12:10."

I didn't think too much about it but wrote it down to look up when I got home later. I didn't really know anything about the Bible. I was surprised—or maybe a little shocked—by what I read. 1 Corinthians 12 was about the diversity of gifts.

1 Corinthians 12:10a says: "To another the working of miracles; to another prophecy; to another discerning of spirits; to another diverse kinds of tongues; to another the interpretations of tongues."

I felt very emotional after reading this and felt sure that I was on my right path and that what religious beliefs I had were not a conflict to what I was doing. I felt that God or the angels or something divine had given John this message for me.

Summer came, and the camp opened for the season. John would do the gallery readings a few times during the summer. I loved going to watch him work; I was amazed by his gifts and kindness. One particular night, I was getting information and hearing spirits. I would hear something in my head and then John would say it. I was blown away—what amazing validation! He would ask me if I had anything for anyone. While sitting in my chair in the audience, I would gingerly give messages I was hearing. I was very nervous. I hadn't yet learned to trust that what I was getting was accurate. Several times, John looked at me and smiled, saying, "I was just getting that." I drove home that night on cloud nine.

I really am *getting real messages.*

There was another time at a church service that John said, "Melissa will give some messages now."

I stayed seated and shook my head. He had the whole congregation encouraging me to try. He was so pushy but in a very loving way. I stood in front of the group and was shaking so badly. *What if I don't get anything? What if I'm wrong?* All those self-doubt thoughts were in my way.

John smiled and said, "Just see what you get—they won't let you down."

I nodded and listened and immediately heard, *Go to the woman in the yellow dress.*

I looked up, and a couple rows back, there was a woman in a yellow dress. My voice slightly trembling, I asked if I could give her a message.

She smiled and said, "Yes, please."

I do not remember what I said, but she nodded and smiled. She understood the message. Then I read a few more, and it went well. I didn't like the fact that John was pushing me to do this before I felt ready, but I can honestly say that if it weren't for John Davidson, I would not be the medium I am today and would probably still be sitting in my seat, doubting what I receive.

At that point, I was still wishing to "see" visions. I could hear spirits and feel them, but I wanted clairvoyance. During one class, John was doing a guided meditation and he guided us to a church using our imagination. I could typically see what he was describing as if I were watching a movie in my head. I saw the church and saw a guide come in that John said would be there.

I asked the guide about seeing, and he said, *You are.*

I said, *No, this is a guided meditation, and it's my imagination.*

My guide said, *Melissa, John didn't describe what I look like or the details that you are seeing. You are seeing.*

Wow, how dumb am I? I had been seeing every time we went into mediation and when Aunt Freda would give me visions, but I expected to see with my eyes like when they show spirits on TV. That's how I thought I was supposed to see them. I can see spirit like that sometimes, but it is rare and more like a faded image. It's more of a flash of my imagination like a daydream when I "see." I now could hear, feel, and see visions from the spirit realm.

John was also the president of the Florence Scripture Church in Fairfield, which opened after the camp had closed for the season. There were several times that he asked me to give messages. It was only a few people each time, but I was gaining confidence.

This is where I met Debbie Locke. She was a medium who served the church. She gave wonderful inspirational talks, but her mediumship was amazing! She was quick and accurate, and I was blown away at how she worked and made it look so easy.

The following year in 2002, I had been through my divorce and my mediumship was still progressing. I took classes with John Davidson at Madison Spiritualist camp again during the summer. Fall was getting cold, and we could no longer meet at Madison for classes. I was disappointed. I was going to miss working with the other people in my class and with John. Later in the winter, John informed us that Debbie Locke was going to be teaching classes at her house in Canaan. I was signed up in a heartbeat. I aspired to be able to work like Debbie Locke.

When we started Debbie's class, there were four of us. It was very evident that Debbie and her guides were helping to bring me to the next level. She introduced me to Grey Wolf.

She said, "You have a Native American guide. His name is Grey Wolf, and he is very protective of you. He is saying that he will be working with you. He is very handsome."

I smiled and thought, *Well, who doesn't want a protective and handsome guide?* There will be more about Grey Wolf later in this book, but he and I started to work together. I could feel the protective and loving energy around me.

I also was working with another guide, Shud (pronounced Shoed). He and Grey Wolf would work with me together at times. When we were joking around, I would hear and feel them laugh. I would feel a tickle in my belly as if I were about to giggle. I was very entertaining to them. They heard all my thoughts. I can be sarcastic at times with the thoughts in my head. I believe I get it from my Irish grandmother, Ruth. It was like having friends there anytime I wanted to talk. We continued to work on developing my mediumship.

I realized at a point that I was still was holding myself back after some challenging experiences (which are explained in another story) I had had before taking classes. I felt protected but was always a little worried about opening up completely. Debbie would encourage me, but she knew I was holding myself back. I felt like the angels had to work to get the negative energies away from me during that time of struggle—I was afraid it would happen again.

Debbie started the classes with a meditation every week. One week, during the opening meditation, I was confused by what I was seeing. I could usually see what she described. If we were going down a path in the woods or wherever she described, I saw it in detail. This time, I didn't see anything but darkness. I saw myself surrounded by darkness; it was a little unnerving. But then I saw gold lights that I knew were angels falling down and forming a circle around me. I felt blessed and safe. It was very comforting. I truly felt like it was to let me know not to worry.

When the meditation was over, Debbie looked at me and, before she said anything else, said, "Melissa, I have to tell you—there is a circle of angels around you."

I was incredulous. Not only did I see it, but so did Debbie. I need big neon signs of validation, and this was a big one.

As if that weren't enough (because it wasn't, I always need more signs . . . I must exhaust them at times), my twin sister stopped by to give me a gift a few weeks later. It wasn't our birthday, it wasn't anywhere near Christmas, and we don't typically buy each other random gifts.

She handed me a small box and said, "I saw this, and you had to have it."

I opened the box and it was a jewelry pin. I almost fell over when I saw what it was. It was a circle of little gold and silver angels. It was a circle of angels. I hugged her and told her the story. It was so amazing. I was feeling truly blessed.

First Reading

Before I had taken development classes and while I was continuing to use divination tools, I had started to feel like I was hearing Spirit better. I at least had given my husband some messages that had come true. I could hear certain things clearly, but some of what I was hearing was like I was listening to a voice that was muffled. I was feeling and sensing more, as well. I knew what the spirits were saying without hearing completely. Sometimes it was a process of repeating what I thought I'd heard, then asking if that's what they said and hearing a "yes" or a "no" answer and listening more intently. I would focus on where I would feel the energy around me.

I had encouraged my husband to look for other jobs. He wasn't happy where he was working. At one point, he had applied for a position with an oil company in the area. He was an accountant and they had an opening in their financial department.

I asked about it and I heard, *He will get the job.* I knew he would. It was beyond just hearing it.

I told him, "I'm getting that you will get the job." He looked skeptical when I told him why I knew that. He was then called for an interview.

I again told him, "You will get the job." He did. They were right.

Our marriage was really rocky at this point, he truly did not understand what I was doing with the mediumship and was very skeptical. Quite frankly, I believed he was scared.

One day, he left the house without saying anything to me. He always seemed mad at me. After he left, I asked Spirit, *Where did he go?*

I heard, *He went to lunch with a friend.*

After asking which friend, I determined that it was his friend Steve, who was a lawyer. He and his wife, Erica, had become good friends to us, and we would spend time together occasionally. Matt came back to the house about an hour and half later.

I said, "Where'd did you go?"

He said, "Does it matter?"

I said, "You went to lunch with Steve, didn't you?"

His jaw dropped. He asked, "How did you know that?"

In an obviously annoyed tone, I said, "How do you think I know that? What I do is real—they told me."

He shook his head and walked upstairs. It was so frustrating to live with someone who didn't understand and made me feel crazy.

One night, I was sitting in the kitchen and started having a conversation with a guide. This particular one is very funny, and he would make me laugh. I was hearing him as if he was standing in front of me talking. I'm not sure I remember what we were "talking" about, but it was very funny. I laughed out loud as Matt walked in the room. In his defense, picture your wife sitting by herself in the near dark and laughing. He sometimes had reason to think I was crazy.

In a not-very-friendly tone, he said, "What's so funny?"

This made me laugh harder, thinking, *He's just going to think I'm crazy.* I tried to sober my expression, and I said, "I was hearing one of my guides, and he made a joke."

His mean response: "Melissa, people that hear voices put their kids in an oven." He was referencing a schizophrenic who had put her kids in the oven because "the voices" were telling her to.

I wasn't smiling anymore; that was very hurtful. I just walked away.

There were a few parents in my day care who were interested in what was happening with me. I wanted to try to do a reading for someone. Rhonda, one of the parents who had two kids in my day care, had asked me to do one for her. I was nervous, but I wanted to put what I could do to the test. We went into a room upstairs, away from everyone. We sat down, and I focused. I felt like I was getting her mother. I told her a few things that she said made sense. But I felt like I wasn't hearing her well. I would check with my guides about what I thought I was hearing from her mother, so it was going kind of slow.

After a few messages, she said, "Melissa, what is my mom's name?"

I asked and tried to listen, but I couldn't quite make out a name. Then I started hearing music. I recognized it as a song by the Goo Goo Dolls.

"I can't seem to get her name, but sometimes I hear music and there is a message in the music," I said. "I'm hearing the song by the Goo Goo Dolls—it's called 'Iris.'"

I started to sing, "'I'd give up forever to touch you, because I know that you feel me somehow—'"

She interrupted me, "Wait! What's the name of that song?" She seemed excited.

I repeated: "'Iris.'"

She said, "Melissa, that is my mother's name!"

I was so excited. I have always had music in my head, and until I started to develop this ability, I didn't realize how many messages I had been receiving over the years. I felt more confident in what I was telling her after that. The reading lasted a little while longer with me receiving messages about her kids and what was coming for her. She thanked me when she left. I think we both felt great about what we had experienced together.

Seeing

Summer 2001
Stetson, Maine

~~~

At this point in my development, I was communicating on a regular basis with my relatives who had passed. At first, I really wasn't sure what my family thought when I gave messages to them. I can understand skepticism from friends and family who knew me all my life, then, at 33 years old I was talking to dead people like they were standing with us (which they were, but how did they know that).

My sister seemed always accepting and supportive. I thought she was the only one. I remember thinking that my older brother was skeptical, and I said something to him about it. It upset him when he heard that I thought he didn't believe me and wasn't supportive of what was happening with me. It was a very emotional moment when he said that he did believe me and supported me. I truly needed to hear him say that. My dad seemed accepting, but again, how do you watch your daughter go from being somewhat normal to talking to dead people in a matter of months?

I had one friend who said she didn't believe me because it took John Edward years to develop his gift, and 'why did I think I could hear them in a matter of months?' Actually, it had been more than a year of doing mediations and exercises at that point, but I was hearing them. It wasn't worth pointing that out. I'm not sure why she thought I would make this up or what my motive would be to lie. I love John Edward and seriously am in awe of him. Maybe I have always had a crush on him ever since I saw "Crossing Over" for the first time. I would never compare what I was doing to what he had accomplished. She knocked my confidence off kilter a bit by saying that. I will never be as amazing as John Edward, but I was hearing them.

My family has always gotten together on Sundays. As kids, we would be at my dad's parents' house in the mornings and my mom's parents' house in the evenings. My mom's sister and her family would be there every Sunday, as well. We grew up with our four cousins; it was a houseful. We were always close to our family. Family dinners happened at my parents' house after the grandparents were older and it was too much for them or after they passed to Spirit. In the summers, it would be at my parents' camp in Stetson on the lake. It later became their retirement home. It was beautiful there. One of my favorite spots in the world is the rock by the lake where I'd sit; I would go there to think. Many times, during the years of my second marriage, I would drive down to the lake and sit on the rock after a fight with him. That rock has seen me excited and happy about things or absolutely heartbroken. I would feel better after sitting there even if it was only for a few minutes.

Most Sundays, at this point, we were joined by the relatives who had passed. I can remember us having conversations and hearing Aunt Freda or her brother, my paternal grandfather, Howard, making comments and joining in. I would say, "Gramp is saying this," or "Aunt Freda is saying this," or something from whoever happened to have joined us at a particular moment. My family would react with a laugh or a comment back. I was the go-between. Like I said, I think most were on the fence about my sanity—how could they not be?

One day, my dad made a comment about how hot it was outside. Most of us loved the hot weather; in Maine there is such a short summer season.

After Dad's remark, I heard my grandfather say, *Ask your dad about the time it was hot in the car.*

So I repeated that to my father, who looked back at me, confused.

I could feel my grandfather laughing. I said, "Dad, whatever it is, he thinks it's funny."

My dad said, "Oh, I bet he's talking about the time when I opened a hot tube of adhesive and it bubbled out and went everywhere."

I suddenly saw it in my head. I could see my father in the back seat of the car, taking the tube out from where it had been sitting near the back window. He looked about 7 years old and was wearing jeans and a white t-shirt. I could even see that he was kind of panicked about the adhesive was bubbling out and not being able to put the cover back on.

My eyes huge, I looked at my father and said, "Dad, were you wearing jeans and a white t-shirt?"

He replied, "I don't know, honey, it was a long time ago."

I said, "Dad, were you about 7 years old?"

He looked surprised and said, "Yes—about that, I think."

I said, "Dad, you were in the back seat of the car and the adhesive was in the back window?"

He looked even more taken aback and said, "Yes, the sun shining in on it got it very hot."

I exclaimed, "Holy cow, Dad! I just saw it! Gramp showed it to me like watching a little movie in my head!" I was ecstatic! I was seeing, and I wasn't in a meditation. It was my first real "seeing" vision. I felt the emotion of the scene as if I were there and watching it personally. I think it was that day that my family believed me even more.

John

2001
Carmel, Maine

One summer evening, I went to my friend Cheryl's house. We have been close since we were 13 years old. We met in high school in home economics class. I sat beside her and started talking, and from then on we were inseparable all throughout our high school years. I spent more weekends at her house than I did at my own. We just always had a great time together and had a special bond. I went camping with her family often. That is how we met the man who became her husband; Bruce and his family would camp at the same campground, and we all became friends.

This particular night, they were having a party, which eventually became an annual event—bonfires, food, drinking, and lots of their friends. I arrived about the time that it was getting dark. My husband didn't want to go, but I insisted that I wasn't going to miss my best friends' party. I promised I would leave by midnight to appease him. I knew it would be a battle when I got home but decided that spending time with Cheryl would be worth it.

When I arrived, she was talking to a handsome guy. He had the most gorgeous eyes that lit up when he smiled. She left his side and came to greet me. Cheryl brought me around to introduce me to other people, then went into the house to get more drinks and food. After she left, I noticed that a woman had walked over to the handsome guy who had been sitting alone in a lawn chair by the fire. She was very intoxicated and introduced herself to him. I watched for a few minutes, entertained by her drunken antics. He showed no interest, and she eventually moved away. Cheryl was still busy, so I went over to him.

I mimicked the girl and did exactly what she did, reaching out my hand to him in an exaggerated motion, saying, "Hi, I'm Sarah." I giggled, thinking how funny I was as I had totally nailed the imitation.

He chuckled and shook my hand, saying, "I don't care what her name is, but what is yours?"

I grinned and said, "Melissa."

He replied: "John."

I plopped down in the lawn chair next to his. He asked how I knew Cheryl, and we chatted about that for a few minutes before we realized that we knew a lot of the same people but had never met.

When I was in high school, I dated guys from the Pittsfield area who went to Maine Central Institute, or MCI, which was a rival to my own high school, Nokomis. I went to the MCI dances and had so many close friends from that high school that were his friends as well. I did not understand how we had never met before. We talked for a few minutes and had a few laughs, then I got up to go find Cheryl. I found her and went into the house to get myself a drink.

When I came back out, John was talking to Cheryl and looked over at me with a disappointed look and said, "I can't believe you are married."

I said, "Sorry."

He said, "You need to get a divorce and marry me."

I was already on my second marriage and it wasn't a good one, so I joked, "Sure—third time's the charm! Where should we get married?"

We laughed about the different locations where we would get married, and he gave me compliments to which I replied, "Okay, Prince Charming, if I weren't married, I would marry you." I smiled and walked away.

During the rest of my time at the party, I felt a tingle every time he looked my way. I was more drawn to him I had ever been to anyone else before. It seemed electrically charged. I would know he was looking at me even with my back to him because of the sensation I would feel physically. At one point, I turned and said, "Stop that."

He gave a dashing grin and said, "Stop what?" But he knew—I was sure that he was feeling it too.

Midnight came way too quickly, and I had to leave. John tried to talk me into staying longer, but I had to go.

I teased him and said, "Well, Prince Charming, I do not have a glass slipper to leave behind—all I have is my sneaker."

He grinned and said, "I'll take it."

I said goodbye to Cheryl and thanked her for a great time, then headed to my car. I got in my car and grinned. John made me feel beautiful, and I had forgotten how great it felt to have someone make you feel like you were something special. I remember thinking, *I'll probably never see him again, but I'll never forget him.*

I got home to find my husband very annoyed that it was so late, even though it was our agreed upon time. I went to bed before he could ruin my night.

After that, Cheryl would mention John in passing after seeing him at their mutual friends' parties and such, but she never mentioned him talking about me. I wouldn't have really cared except I didn't want to feel like I had made up the whole tingling connection I had felt—I wanted it to be real. I had never experienced anything like it before and wasn't sure why it had happened.

A year later, the time for Cheryl's annual party came around. I had a wedding to photograph that day but decided that I would stop by afterwards.

I walked into the house to look for Cheryl and there was John, smiling that gorgeous smile and saying, "Where have you been? I've been waiting for you for a year!"

I grinned back but was too stunned by his comment to think of a clever comeback, so I said, "I was photographing a wedding."

We chatted and laughed together for most of the party. We were sober in comparison to some of the other folks there; it was very entertaining. I found myself telling him about all of the interesting things that were happening with me—the "feelings" I had that ended up being right. I also told him about the tingles I had felt every time he looked at me a year ago, wondering if it was a past life thing. He was more interested than probably anybody else had been at this point other than Nan.

This time when I left the party, he followed me to my car. He expressed what a good time he'd had and I agreed. Upon reaching my car, we faced each other, neither of us really wanting the night to end.

He said, "I can't let you leave again without doing this." He leaned in and gave me a sweet little kiss. It was so tender and caring. It was a beautiful kiss that I felt all the way down to my toes. Not knowing what to say, I got in my car, and he watched me drive away.

I thought about my marriage on the drive back home—how much negativity there was about the experiences I was having and the almost-constant insults and anger that were now also being directed towards my kids. I couldn't even feel guilty about enjoying the kiss.

When I arrived back at my house, there was—of course—another fight. I just heard him yelling and didn't respond. I was exhausted. It was exhausting being in this marriage, but I was determined not to put my kids through another divorce.

John and I had exchanged email addresses at the party. I sent him an email a few days after the party. My day care kids were napping, and I had a few minutes to myself. I was scrolling through the TV channels when I felt an intense tingle in my belly—I knew that John had responded to my email. I turned on my computer, and, sure enough, the message had arrived just as I was feeling the tingle. I thought that was so cool.

We emailed occasionally after that. He was always interested to hear about metaphysical and spiritual things so when they happened, I would email him. It was nice to have someone supportive and interested. One time, we discussed the kiss.

He explained how drawn to me he had been and how connected he felt to me. He said, "That's why I kissed you, I needed you to know that I felt it too."

All the little tingles that happened every time he messaged me assured me of that connection.

Months went by and we continued to email occasionally. It was around this time that I got sick, my liver failed, and I got divorced. I moved out of the house and back into the mobile home I had owned before we had gotten married.

At this point, it was getting near the time for the annual party. We met up at the party and had a great time. We ended the party with some very passionate kisses and made plans to meet another time.

We talked on the phone. He lived an hour and half away from me, and with my two kids' and his two kids' schedules, it was hard to find time to see him. We finally made a plan to get together at his house. Before I went to his house, I had a dream or a vision of what it looked like. It was so strange, when I walked into his house it was exactly like I had seen it; it was like I had been there before.

I told him this and said, "The only thing is, I thought I would walk into the kitchen and face the living room. It's just opposite from what I saw."

He grinned and said, "Melissa, no one comes in the front door. Everyone comes in through the kitchen entrance."

We had a great time that night, but I don't believe either of us were ready for anything serious. I was still healing from the divorce.

The connection I felt to him was so strong. There were a few times I called him with "feelings" about things that would happen or had happened that I would randomly get. Each time he validated what I was feeling or what was going on.

Months later, I was driving to church in Fairfield and I couldn't get him off my mind—this time it didn't feel good. During the church service, I was uncomfortable and worried about him. After church, I was having lunch with a friend, and I felt pain in my chest and couldn't get John out of my head. It was so strong. I left the restaurant and called him.

He answered, "Hello?"

I said, "John, why can't I get you off my mind, why does my chest hurt, and why do I feel like crying?"

He said, "Wow, you are dead on again. I can't explain because the girls are here with me, but just know that I just left the hospital. They are running some tests for pains in my chest."

I was dumbfounded and worried, but I was getting that he was going to be okay. He called later to explain, and I had this feeling that I could help him—that I could do a healing for him. He seemed a little hesitant but agreed. We decided I would go to see him later in the week.

When I got to his house, I remember feeling that he needs to know that this was real and that it would work. I had put a crystal in my pocket. I wasn't sure why until then. I went in and hugged John. I didn't have a lot of time, so I had him sit in a chair. I knelt in front of him and put my right hand on his chest with the crystal between my palm and his chest. I had my other hand on his. I took my deep breaths to clear my mind and visualized white light coming down through me and into his chest. I felt the energy flow, and I felt as if I were being lifted up. It's hard to explain, but it was a sensation of rising like my energy was reaching up to connect. I felt my body get hot and my hands tingle. When I was done, I caught the crystal with my hand, and it was very hot—a lot hotter than how it would be if you just held it in your hand.

I said, "John, that was some great energy—feel how hot this got?!"

He said, "Wow, that is hot!" He said that he could feel how hot my hands had gotten while touching him during the healing. We chatted for a few moments and caught up on what was happening in our lives. He was just starting to date someone. And even though we stayed friends and would message occasionally, we started to distance.

A few years later, I was in a deep meditation and asked about the connection that John and I had had. I was hearing that John and I were supposed to have met in high school. We would have been married soon after graduating. We were supposed to have two girls, and I was going to drown in a lake at 34. But somehow, we didn't meet—maybe because of who I was dating in high school or maybe because of choices he made, too. There were too many facts that made that seem very real. Because John and I had so many mutual friends, we spent time at the same places but somehow never met. We both had two girls. He had not ever married. He lived on a lake. My liver failed, and I had my near-death experience at 34.

I heard that by the time we had met and I was available after my divorce, he was supposed to have already lost me and already be at the point on his path where he'd have continued to live his life without me. He was due to meet the woman he ended up marrying. But I am grateful for the time I had with him and will never forget the connection. We've lost touch, but I always wonder how he is doing and hope he is happy.

Archangels, Finding My Strength

Winter 2002
Carmel, Maine

Months after my miracle healing, I had an amazing experience. My mediumship had really started to develop into a constant contact with the spiritual realm. There was always a conversation going on in my head with someone on the other side even during a conversation with another human here on the Earth plane.

At this point, I was divorced. My girls and I were living in my mobile home on some land not far from where we had lived when I was married. The land I owned had beautiful views but also had a major power line that crossed the front part of the property. The house was about 50 feet from this electrical energy source. Not only was I more sensitive to energies from my healing, but the energy source of the power line gave spirits a constant supply from which to draw to allow for communication. Most mediums have guides who have established protection around them prior to working with spirits. I had opened up on my own before taking classes and did not have a clue about protecting myself. Because of the power source and my sensitivity, I was like an open phone booth for the other side—they did not have to establish connection with one of my guides and most surpassed them. It got a little overwhelming just like John Davidson had predicted. Quite frankly, I caused most of my own issues by talking to any spirit that chose to stop and say hi. I was not prepared for the amount of attention I received from the other side.

If I was focused on something else and not paying attention to the conversations in my head, I would get a tingling sensation in my abdomen to get my attention from the spirits. I would feel this sensation and know to listen.

On a day like any other, I was in my kitchen; I'll never forget this moment. I felt an intense sensation like electricity running through my body. I felt a pressure around my head as if I was wearing a tight helmet. I had to sit down.

I was a little nervous as I asked in my head, *Who is this?*

I heard, *Archangel Michael.*

I immediately thought, *No, it isn't,* thinking it was a spirit just teasing me. Why would an archangel talk to me?

Then I heard, *Yes, Melissa, it is.*

I again thought, *No,* refusing to believe this to be true.

I heard, *Melissa, think about how your body is reacting to my energy.*

I took a moment. It was true. There had never been this intense feeling when connecting with anything before.

I was awestruck and was in disbelief at the same time.

Michael explained that there was work for me to do. He said, *There is a reason why we intervened and allowed you to stay on the Earth plane. We have work for you to do but the interference and influence with the spiritual realm is prohibiting you from moving forward into this plan. You agreed to stay there longer; you agreed to assist us with helping people. We are asking you to stop talking to all the spirits who contact you. You are not being allowed to hear what you need to hear because of the distraction of those who seek your attention. We would like you to stop talking with them and work with only guides and angels from this moment on.*

At that time, I didn't completely understand. I later realized that I am very influenced by what I hear subconsciously, whether I was aware of the communication or not. It was a problem.

I realized later that I would cry or feel like I wanted to laugh and not know why. I remember one night I was just sitting and watching TV, and I started to cry.

My daughter asked, "Mommy, why are you crying?"

I remember saying, "I don't know honey—someone is sad somewhere."

I was feeling spirits even if I wasn't actively talking to them. I was responding to them without realizing. Sometimes things would come out of my mouth, and I would think, *Why did I say that?* I was beginning to understand what Michael was telling me about the influence. There was so much more that I either hadn't noticed or didn't mind. My sleep was being interrupted. Spirits were waking me up by talking to me and asking me to pass on messages, sometimes to people I barely knew. My energy was on high all the time. I lost a lot of weight. I actually had people tell me that they were worried about me, saying that I looked "too thin." I was 10 to 15 pounds lighter than my usual mid-130s. I had attributed it to the divorce and the emotions and stress around that, but now I understood that it wasn't just that.

While explaining what was happening and how much involvement there was, one of my guides said, *Melissa, when you cry, all of heaven cries; when you laugh, all of heaven laughs.*

I understood now. When I was sad, it felt so much stronger because I was feeling all of "their" sadness too. When I found something funny, it was way funnier.

There were serious bouts of depression. I knew logically that there was nothing to feel down about, but I couldn't bring myself out of it for the first time in my life. I've always been able to get over things that upset me quickly. I had never let anything keep me down for long. I was starting to worry about my sanity. I know I wasn't in the best state to take care of my kids. I was beyond exhausted; I would fall asleep in the blink of an eye. Once, I even fell asleep in my driveway and scared my kids half to death. I was supposed to have picked them up, and a friend drove them home to find me asleep on the wheel of my car. Occasionally, I would start to fall asleep while driving and as my eyes closed, I would feel an electric jolt to wake me up. It would come out of nowhere. I know the angels were watching over me and keeping me safe.

Michael started working with me. I would meditate and clear my mind. They were trying to create a barrier of protection around me. I tried to keep my mind quiet and allow it. It was a long process of days of meditations and connecting with his energy. The archangel Gabriel assisted as well. His energy felt similar, but I got to know which one of them was working with me. It consisted of many hours of trying to keep my mind clear when I was off from work or my kids were asleep or occupied.

One day, I heard, *Uriel will be working with you now. He helps solve problems.*

I questioned, *Uriel?*

Yes, Melissa. Uriel. U-R-I-E-L.

I had never heard of Uriel, but I accepted that this angel would be trying to help me.

A couple of weeks later, I went to a bookstore. I, of course, went to the metaphysical section. A book about angels caught my attention. I grabbed it off the shelf and just allowed the pages to open in my hands. The page it stopped on had a title: "Uriel."

I thought, *Wow, I'm not crazy. I didn't make this up.* I read that he was an archangel and is known as 'the problem solver.'

Days and weeks went by. I struggled more, even though the angels were working with me. I was told that it would take time to create a barrier. I started to decline even more—I was stressed, worried, and sad; all the things I've never really had experienced before on this level. I had no control over what was happening to me. Life became difficult. For the first time, I couldn't pull myself out of it. I asked why this was happening. I trusted and believed everything.

Why—if there are angels helping me—are they allowing this? Am I being punished? Am I being taught a lesson, if so, what is it?

I did not understand at the time. Things had been easy in my life before this. That's not to say that I hadn't faced difficulty or heart break—two divorces, being a single mom, financial struggles, etc.—it was just that I had faith and truly believe everything happened for a reason and it was to get me to a better place. Perhaps I had judged those who struggled with things that seemed minor and nothing to be upset about or couldn't let things go like I did. I saw it as weak. No longer did I judge anyone's struggles. I couldn't control mine anymore.

I met a man named Glen, and we became friends. He had something very special about him. I truly believe he was led to me. After getting to know him better, I shared my secret. At this point, there were not many people who knew I was a medium. I told him many stories. He was interested and listened and was supportive.

One night, I told him that I would never hurt myself because of my kids, but if I got hit by a bus the next day, I would be thankful that it was over; I was exhausted. I felt like it took everything I had to get through a day.

Glen told me, "You are too young to feel that way. At 36, you should be experiencing the best of life." He thought for a moment then asked if I would be open to seeing the minister at his church. He stated, "He and I have been friends for years. Let me talk to him and set up a meeting."

I agreed. I was hopeful that he could answer some questions for me.

A week went by. Glen called and said that he had set up an appointment with his friend who was a Baptist minister. On the way there, I had a feeling and said to Glen, "This is going to be about him—this isn't so much for me. He does what I do or did."

Glen scoffed and said, "No, listen, I've known this guy for 20 years. I would know."

I said, "Okay," but thought, *We will see.*

We arrived at the church. The minister was nice, but I felt that he wasn't going to understand. We talked for a bit, and then he proceeded to tell me that what I was doing was of the devil and I needed to stop immediately. "I know what I'm talking about. I used to be in a band, and I did drugs, and I did what you do. It was all work of the devil."

I looked at my friend with a knowing (okay, maybe an 'I told you so') look on my face.

He looked shocked and said, "I don't know if you believe her, but, man, on the way over here, she said exactly what you just said."

He said, "Tricks of the devil."

It was strange that this didn't upset me. I wanted him to see that it wasn't like that—maybe he needed to believe me so that he would know that he was going to be okay.

I said, "Why would the devil allow me to see angels and give people messages of hope that help restore their faith?"

I told him about a few experiences I had with angels and spirits. Then I asked him to explain why there was a miracle that happened to me when I should have died. I wanted to convince him that love and the angels are more powerful than anything bad. I don't think I did, but what I didn't realize at the time was that this was helping me. I believed in what I was saying. I had had some amazing experiences, and I was truly blessed to see what I see.

After we left the church, my friend apologized to me and said, "I'm sorry I doubted you."

I cried and just felt so tired. He took me home.

The next time I saw Glen, I was convinced that I was crazy. I had some weird experiences after which I really questioned my sanity. I believed that there was something bad causing my problems. I believed that I was being haunted by an angry spirit. I was scared, and things were happening to me that caused my fear to grow. I was letting my fear of what was happening to me control me. I was feeding the fear, and the depression was becoming worse.

"Why is this happening?" I said to Glen after I explained what was going on—that is a story for another time.

He responded, "I think you have a chemical imbalance; I think we should go see a doctor today." It was Sunday so he took me to the emergency room at a local hospital.

When they were checking me in, I didn't even know what to say.

"My friend thinks I may have a chemical imbalance; I'm having some strange experiences."

I cautiously admitted that I had been seeing and hearing things that scared me. I truly thought that I was ready for some medication and a padded room. They put me in a room. The doctor came in and asked me what was going on. I asked him questions.

"Could my mind be tricking me into feeling something touch me when there is nothing there? Or could my mind be creating voices in my head or causing physical sensations."

He looked at me and said, "Not really. I think you should talk to a counselor."

They called a counselor, and we waited a while for him to arrive. He finally arrived and introduced himself as he came in the room. He sat in a chair in the corner. Glen sat beside me and was wonderfully supportive. The counselor asked, "What is going on? Describe what is happening to you."

For the following four hours, I told story after story of experiences that I had experienced—some absolutely beautiful, some that scared me, some that helped strangers, some that seemed unbelievable. As I talked, I looked him in the eyes and told him what I was feeling, what I heard, and how strangers reacted when I told them something there was no way for me to know that helped them in some way. I also told him about the fun ones where someone would say, "Oh my God, you are freaking me out right now!"

The more stories I told, the more I cried but the more I was convinced that I wasn't crazy. How could I talk to someone I'd never met before and give them messages from a loved one or a guide that they understood and validate? I had to have gotten the message from a spirit—my mind couldn't come up with the knowledge on its own. I felt an angel in the room with me allowing all of what I had been afraid to talk about come out.

When I was done, I asked for medicine for a headache. I think crying so much caused the awful headache I was experiencing.

The counselor looked at me and said, "We can get you some aspirin." Then he said, "Melissa, I don't even know what to say. You are not crazy. Just by you questioning that is really proof that you are not. Crazy people don't know they are crazy." He continued with, "I believe what you are telling me and quite frankly you have me questioning my own spiritual beliefs. Your stories are clear—you describe them in detail without hesitation. You are being truthful because you are looking me in the eyes. I do not know how to help you. I am going to talk to some of my colleagues who have more experience with spiritual matters. I will try to find someone to help you." As he left, he said that someone would call in a few days.

Even though my head was pounding with the emotional crying, I felt better. My friend was blown away. He said, "I will never question your gift again. I had no idea at all of what you have experienced. Those were some amazing stories."

For the first time in a long time, I felt empowered. When I was speaking with the minister and the counselor, I realized how strong my faith was and how I know my truths. By allowing myself to experience the worst of the human emotions, sadness, fear, and pain, I was able to find my strength. I could handle this. I wasn't crazy. The angel in the room had made me realize that they were still with me and looking after me. I never did hear back from a counselor, but I didn't need one. Over the next few weeks, I took it on. I wasn't backing down. I was not allowing fear. I called on the angels and felt their presence any time I started to question or worry. I released all negative thoughts. I was strong. I was a medium. I was NOT crazy.

Diego

March 2004
Argentina

In 2003, I was "shut off." My mediumship had become so overwhelming that I couldn't sleep. There was constantly a spirit talking to me, even if I was having a normal, human conversation at the same time. I tried to shut it down, but I was still being woken up at night by spirits who asked me to pass on messages. My energy was on "screech" all the time, even with the angels trying to help block me. When I tried to do readings, it was as if a radio was flipping through stations rapidly. I heard little bits from a lot of spirits but couldn't make sense of any of it. My guides said that they talked to the angels and the only solution was to shut me off. I was asked to get rid of anything spiritual. I was told that I could never do this again. I argued back and pleaded for them not to take it away. In the end, I didn't have a choice. I had to do what they asked.

I was broken-hearted. I cried. I felt so alone, and for the first time in years, everything was quiet. Imagine that for a couple years, you constantly hear spirits to now hearing nothing in your head. I knew they were still there—I just couldn't hear them or feel them anymore. I felt like I was being punished even though I knew it was to protect me. The interesting thing was, it was like my mediumship had never happened. People used to talk to me almost daily about it, but now it was never mentioned.

My sister and my friend Cheryl were the only people who asked, "You're not doing readings anymore?"

I said, "No," and no more questions were asked.

I had been taking classes with Debbie Locke, and she didn't even call to see why I wasn't coming to class. "They" told her I suppose. It was just wiped completely from people's minds.

I started chatting online I think to fill the void. Diego and I met online on an instant messenger one evening in 2003. He was looking to find out information about something that had happened in Carmel, California, but got me in Carmel, Maine instead. He was from Rosario, Argentina. At that point in my life, I was fascinated with chatting with people from all over the world. I chatted with people from England, Turkey, Russia, Egypt, Tunisia, and more. I was intrigued by the different cultures. Through Yahoo messenger, the world opened up to me.

That night, I explained to Diego that Carmel, California was across the continent from me. Diego had a great sense of humor, and I enjoyed chatting with him so much that first time that I looked forward to chatting with him again.

It was a fun pastime for me to chat online. Diego and I chatted most nights. Then we started chatting during the day when the kids in my day care were napping. That led to using the webcam and actually seeing each other as we typed. Back then, the connection was not good enough for us to talk. We attempted a few times, but it was unclear and broken up. He joked about me coming to visit; he would be my Argentinian boyfriend. Just for fun, I looked at websites, but ticket prices were over $1,200, which I couldn't afford as a single mom. But I would have loved to go meet him in person and see another country.

We became close. Seeing him every day for an hour or so on the computer felt like he was coming to see me every day in my house. I looked forward to our chats. He was always interested in my day and told me about his.

I started getting signs. Diego and I were chatting one night about the song "I Still Haven't Found What I'm Looking For" by U2, and the next morning, I woke up to that song playing on my alarm clock radio. I started to see things about Argentina on the local news. Argentina would come up in conversations randomly. Diego continued to invite me to come see him.

One evening in January as we were chatting, I got the tingle that I used to feel when spirits were trying to get my attention. I listened, but heard nothing. Diego was asking me again to come visit him. His brother was getting married in March, and he wanted me to be his date.

I typed, "Ha ha, I would if I could afford it."

I felt the tingle again. Still I heard nothing. I had a thought to check ticket prices again. I did. To my shock, they had dropped down to $600. I could put that on a credit card. I let the thought go, but I was still messaging with Diego and told him about the price drop.

He said, "Baby." He had started calling me that a while ago. "You should come, you can stay with me at my parents' house. I will come get you in Buenos Aires; my parents have an apartment there. You wouldn't have to pay for a place to stay."

Without really thinking, I found myself booking the ticket. I was so excited in that moment, but then I thought, *What did I just do?* Panic set in. I wished so bad to hear that this was what "they" wanted me to do. I felt that all the signs about Argentina and the connection I had felt with Diego was all a part of what my guides were encouraging me to do. I truly felt like this was a leap of faith. I need to go and trust that there was a reason.

My family did not take the news well. They thought that I was out of my mind to go to a foreign country to meet a man I had only been chatting with online. Even writing this now, I realize how crazy it must have seemed to them. I couldn't explain it to them beyond the fact that I felt like I needed to go.

My dad said, "I wish you wouldn't go."

It upset me to disappoint my dad, but I explained, "Dad, I feel like I need to go. I can't explain it. I need to take this leap of faith."

They thought I was going because I was in love with Diego. At this point, I considered him a friend that I cared about but nothing more. Along with all the signs to go, I really wanted a vacation and I knew that I would enjoy being with him.

I made arrangements for my girls, took time off, and scrambled to get a passport. I had to pay extra to make sure my passport was here in time—not a thought I'd had when I booked the ticket.

March arrived quickly. I was nervous but so excited. Diego was wonderful through our chats—sweet and supportive, and he always had a sense of humor. I flew from Bangor to New York. From there I took a 10-hour flight into Buenos Aires; it was an overnight flight, very long and in a filled plane. It wasn't really a good place to sleep. I dozed off and on in between other passengers on either side of me. I was tired but excited. Before the plane landed, I went into the small airplane bathroom to touch up my hair and makeup. I wanted to look as best I could after a night of very little sleep.

My stomach was all butterflies as I got off the plane. I spotted him immediately. Our eyes met and a big smile took over his face. He came right over to me and landed a very passionate kiss on my lips. He was even more attractive in person and that kiss made my knees weak. He took my hand and my luggage, and we took a cab to his parents' apartment. I was fascinated as I looked out the window. Buenos Aires is such a beautiful city. March was near the end of their summer. I left 20-degree weather, and there it was in the 80s—everything was so green and lush.

When we arrived at the apartment building, Diego told me that this is where his parents live most of the time but they were not home. I would meet them later. We went into the apartment, and he introduced me to the housekeeper. She approached me and kissed me on both cheeks. I was a little surprised. Diego explained that it is a part of their culture to do that. I felt so welcomed.

He showed me around the beautiful apartment, and we sat and talked. I felt so close to this man that I had just met physically for the first time. I trusted him completely.

I was exhausted. He took me to the bedroom, and we lay down. One thing led to another and we became intimate. I was in love with this man from first sight. He was so tender and loving and romantic. Argentina became heaven.

The next day, I met his brother, Damian. Damian kissed my cheeks and said that it was nice to meet me. He then said, "Melissa, say this word, *pelotudo*." It was something like that, I'm not exactly sure it was so long ago.

I repeated it and said, "What does that mean?"

He said, "It means 'asshole.'"

I laughed and joked that it may come in handy. Diego laughed. We left and he showed me around Buenos Aires. It truly was a beautiful city. We went to lunch and walked around a park and checked out a beautiful church. There were statues of angels everywhere. It was a perfect day. Everything beautiful, and I was in love.

The next day, we traveled a few hours to Rosario to the house where he lived. They were doing renovations, but it was a beautiful house. We went through a gate and a little garden area that led into the house. He introduced me to his dog, Connie, and three cats. He loved his animals, and the dog was so well trained.

He took me sightseeing at places in Rosario. We had a great time getting to know each other better as we explored his city. Everyone he introduced me to was so friendly and kissed my cheeks in greeting. I loved this culture. The food was amazing. Argentina is known for its meat. One night, Diego made me *asado*, similar to our barbecue. I loved the *facturas*, which are Argentinian pastries—I ate them every day. We would nap in the afternoons and have dinner around 10 or 11 o'clock at night.

I met his mother and father. His mom, Ana, was an English teacher; that is why Diego knew English so well. She and I hit it off immediately. Our first conversation was about angels. I knew that part of the reason I had to come to Argentina was to meet her. She was a beautiful woman inside and out. She made me feel so welcome. I believe she could see that I loved her son and accepted me right away.

While I was there, I found myself talking about things in my past that I had been holding on to and hadn't realized still bothered me. I talked about them with Diego, and his love and support made everything seem so much better. The trip ended up being so healing for me.

He took me to an island beach on the river. It was beautiful. We shared a beer and swam in the water. There was music playing, and I was standing in the water in front of Diego and moving with the music. He gave me a gorgeous smile and said, "Baby, I like drunk blondes."

I laughed and threw my arms around his neck and kissed him.

Diego made up songs and sang them to me. He loved to comment that I was "a clever blonde." He was the perfect gentleman. Between Diego and his dad, I didn't open a door, carry anything, or get out of a car without a hand offered to me. I was treated like a princess.

The day came when we were to travel a few hours to the city of Parana where his brother was getting married. We took a double-decker bus. We listened to music and talked all the way there. My time with Diego was fun. We laughed a lot, and we both had a sarcastic, teasing sense of humor.

We arrived at our hotel. Diego got us checked in, and we went to our room and unpacked our things. I sprawled out on the bed to relax.

He turned and said, "Baby, do you have your clothes ready for the morning? The civil ceremony is early."

It struck me as if I had been hit with a physical blow. It was the most intense déjà vu I had ever experienced. I had seen this all before—exactly what he'd said, where he was standing, and how I was lying on the bed. I knew at that moment that Diego and I would only be together for this short time while I was in Argentina. It was so powerful that I started to cry. Diego, not knowing what had hit me, was immediately concerned.

He said, "Baby, what is the matter?"

I moved away from him and said, "We will not be together. This is only while I am here, and I am so sad because I have fallen in love with you."

He held me and said, "Baby, you *loco*! No one knows their fate, we decide our future."

I said, "I know with everything in me. This is not meant to be more than this."

He held me and said, "Baby, don't worry."

Even though I wasn't hearing spirits at this time, I had a knowledge that came from the déjà vu that I cannot to this day explain. I tried to believe Diego. I pushed it out of my mind and got my dress ready for the next day.

We got up early and went to watch the civil ceremony at the local official's office. The church ceremony was later that night; it was beautiful. I felt so blessed to witness such a blessed event. The reception was later. When we arrived at the reception, Diego carried my camera case, being the perfect gentleman, as always.

One of his friends walked up to him and was not happy to see me. I wasn't sure why—because I was American, because Diego had a date, I'm not sure. He said something in Spanish to Diego that I didn't understand. I saw the smile leave Diego's face.

I asked Diego, "What did he say?" But Diego just shook his head, not wanting to tell me. I said, "Tell me what he said. I know you are not happy about it."

He said, "He said that you have broad shoulders and you should carry your own things."

Damian's lesson popped into my head, and I looked at him and said, "*Pelotudo.*"

Diego laughed so hard and said, "Baby, that's good."

We had a great time. Diego and I danced slow dances and I danced with his family on fast songs. I was having a blast. The music, the beautiful people, and this man who showed me love and care all made for an incredible night. To be in a foreign country and feel so at home was amazing.

Diego and I left and went back to the hotel. I was so head over heels for this man. Not knowing what would happen in our future didn't matter. I was his and he was mine even if it was just for this moment.

On our ride back to Buenos Aires, his dad drove the car. We stopped at a gas station with a convenience store attached. Diego looked at me and said, "Baby, do you want *facturas?*"

I said, "No, thank you, Diego, I've gained so much weight on this trip."

Diego said very seriously, "Baby, you are already fat. You might as well have them."

I laughed so hard. I had never been called fat before with so much love and humor. Diego's dad did not speak English and asked why we were laughing. When Diego told him, he joined in. I was not fat; I did, however, gain six pounds on the trip. I enjoyed every one of those calories.

When it came time for me to go home, I had such mixed emotions. I couldn't wait to get home to see my girls, but I didn't want to leave Diego. I wanted to trust him that we would be together, but I didn't.

He dropped me off at the airport, and I had to rush. We had arrived later than we'd planned. I didn't have a long good-bye. I quickly kissed him and told him that I loved him, and I rushed away. I was worried about getting through the long line at customs and making my flight. They were calling my name as I got to the gate. I was told that I had just made it, they were about to close the doors. I got settled on the plane for the long flight and the tears started.

Is it possible to continue this with him? Is this it? What will happen with us?

I arrived back in Bangor the next day to 23-degree weather and snow covering my car. I had left Bueno Aires at 9 p.m. and it was 85 degrees. I wanted to go back. I brushed off the snow and made my way home.

My girls were still in school. I dropped my bags in my bedroom and then got on the computer to message Diego that I was home. As the computer was starting, I heard my grandfather—my grandfather who was passed. It was just him, no other voices. He was confirming what I knew about Diego and me. I couldn't believe I was hearing spirits again. I felt excited and blessed but didn't like what my grandfather was telling me.

Within a few days of being back, I was hearing other spirits one at a time, as well. I would have to listen, or "tap in" as I call it, but I could hear them when I did. The trip was what I needed to clear the energies. I believe being away, releasing old wounds, and Diego's love with the help of the angels fixed the problem I had with hearing everything all at once. Unfortunately, they all were confirming that I needed to let Diego go, that I was holding him back from his true path. If I stayed with him, I would keep him from the experiences he was meant to have. I couldn't forget that I was not supposed to still be here. Just because I didn't die didn't mean that I could affect others' paths. I cannot affect the paths of those with whom I come in contact, unless it will not keep them from experiencing what they planned before incarnation.

I messaged Diego and broke up with him. I cried for three days straight. I had never been so broken-hearted over a breakup before. I don't think I was very nice to those spirits that told me to let him go. Sometimes it is so hard to do the right thing, especially when it means letting go of an amazing love.

To this day, Diego and I will occasionally message each other. It may be a year or more in between connecting with him, but I feel the love as if I were back in his arms. It makes me happy and sad at the same time. Ultimately, I was grateful to have such an amazing experience and to have had Diego be mine even for a short time. It was a true, deep love unlike anything else I had experienced.

Grey Wolf

Carmel, Maine

Grey Wolf is one of my spirit guides. He was first presented to me at a class with Debbie Locke. She had seen him with me during one of her classes. She described him as Native American, very handsome, strong, and protective. Leaving Debbie's that night, I was aware of him. I couldn't really hear him or see him at that point. I just felt him.

As time went by, my own meditations helped to raise my vibration, and I soon could hear him. There was something about this connection that felt different than others. I felt a loving energy every time I spoke with him. I didn't completely understand it at that point.

He was guiding and encouraging. The more I worked with him, the more I felt a feeling of love and protection around me. Other spirits would come to me and talk about Grey Wolf and his great love—a love that everyone dreams of having, a true love. He was in love with Orielle on Spirit side.

I would feel Grey Wolf's loving energy around me when I was sad or upset about something. Sometimes lying on my bed crying, I would feel his energy surround me as if he were cradling me in his arms. He would bring me music to comfort me. I would hear "Hero" by Enrique Iglesias in my head.

I can be your hero baby, I can kiss away the pain, I will stand by you forever, you can take my breath away...

I cannot describe how safe and loved I felt when that happened. Yet, I still didn't understand why this guide made me feel like I was special to him.

There was one point that I was told that he wouldn't be able to be near me. It was during the chaos of trying to clear the energies away from me before I was shut off. I felt hurt and pain at hearing this. I realized that it wasn't mine—it was Grey Wolf's. I realized that he loved me more than the love of a spirit guide, but I still didn't understand.

I would hear Shud and Grey Wolf all the time. There was a point when a very uptight spirit came in and told me that I shouldn't joke about sex after I had made a sexual innuendo. I happen to think most things about sex are funny. It is maybe because I still have a teenage boy brain from when I was a 19-year-old boy who died in Vietnam in my last life. The spirit told me it was not appropriate. I told him sex was natural and an expression of love, so how can it be bad? I could "feel" Grey Wolf and Shud laughing as they were listening in on this conversation. I started to giggle then thought, *Stop laughing.*

They hadn't realized how sensitive I had become. I really could literally feel their laughter in my belly like it was my own. What I didn't understand then was that I had to be connected to that energy for them to hear me and for me to hear them. The spirits cannot hear each other talking to me. The other spirit had no idea what was making me laugh or that I was having a conversation with my guide. I had thought that it was like a conference call, but really it was multiple single-line calls. During this time, I heard and felt everything. I was constantly connected. There was no filter, no blocks; I was open for anything that came through.

And then came the time that I was "shut off." It was so quiet and lonely. I missed my daily conversations with Shud and Grey Wolf. Even as I write this, I'm wondering how many people could understand this. It's like talking to a friend daily, then going a year without hearing from them. But instead of a phone, it was in my head—no electronics needed.

After I got back from Argentina, I could hear them again, but it was filtered. I could only occasionally hear from Grey Wolf and Shud. I had other guides. I would ask them questions about what was happening in my life. I had been in love but never the kind you read about in romance novels. My relationships never lasted. I was skeptical about a lasting love, even though I had many examples in my family of what a loving relationship looked like. I had been in love, but it would fade. Diego was the closest thing I could call a storybook romance, but it wasn't on his path to be with me. Then one day, a guide told me that it was not on my path to experience that type of love. That I had a true love on Spirit side, but when we incarnated together, we always found each other.

I was told, *You chose to come to this life and not have him with you. You needed to learn lessons without that love and comfort.* It was also explained that this was to have been a short life, and I was supposed to have died by now and been back to my love on the other side. I still didn't connect the dots.

Then one day, a spirit came in and said that my higher self is called Orielle. A part of our energy stays on the Spirit side that we mediums refer to as our higher selves.

I thought, stunned, *Grey Wolf's Orielle?*

Yes, was the answer I received. I'm not sure why it was a secret although I'm sure it had something to do with us not being able to know everything and not having interference from the other side. It all made sense. I felt his love for me; I felt the protection around me. On a human level, I couldn't really grasp what that love was like, but I definitely felt his love for me.

Years later, I was living with a guy I had been dating for a few years when a strange thing happened. We had been out drinking, and he had more than he should have. We were having sex and it felt different. It felt like he was someone else—he had broader shoulders and was taller. If I kept my eyes closed, I would not have thought it was my boyfriend on top of me. It was so strange. I looked at my boyfriend and he stared into my eyes and said, "I love you so much." The emotion overwhelmed me. I knew this wasn't my boyfriend. He was the "love ya" kind of guy and had never before and never after expressed that depth of emotion. It just wasn't my boyfriend, but I couldn't explain it.

Years later, I was dating another guy. This guy and I had an immediate connection. One night while we were kissing, he said, "I just want to breathe you." I thought that was romantic and felt especially close to him in that moment.

Later this guy said to me, "Who is Grey Wolf, and what has he got to do with me?"

I had mentioned one time that I had a guide named Grey Wolf. The guy had been on a trip and said that he'd seen signs of Grey Wolf everywhere and wasn't sure why. I believe Grey Wolf was working with him. This guy was there when I needed someone, and I think Grey Wolf assisted this connection.

Years later, I was very attracted to this guy from "the County." That's how us Mainers refer to Aroostook County. He and I had a few good dates. One night, standing in my kitchen and kissing me, he said, "I just want to breathe you."

I was stunned. To have another guy say those exact words to me was way beyond coincidence, and who says that anyway? That relationship did not last long after that. He had anger and jealousy issues that I had no use or tolerance for at that point.

The next year I was dating a guy and, initially, there was a great attraction and felt like I was falling for him. One night as we were kissing in my kitchen in almost the exact same spot as the guy before, he says, "I just want to breathe you."

I could have fallen over. I couldn't believe the same words said with the same tone came out of another man's mouth. Seriously, I need big neon signs, and this definitely was one; this was definitely Grey Wolf stepping in with his influence over these men. This relationship turned bad a few months later, but I believe I was supposed to have been in it to help his son.

I believe Grey Wolf can influence the people I am with, either to get me into a relationship or to help me feel a love that has been lacking in my life. I'm not sure what our relationship is like on the other side, but I believe that when it is time to go home, I'll be lovingly greeted by Grey Wolf; I have a very romantic scene in my head of us running into each other's arms. For now, I take comfort in the fact that he is with me, loving me, encouraging me, and helping to protect and guide me.

Denial Guy

2005
Bangor, Maine

—✦—

Being single again, I would go out with my girlfriends on Saturday nights. My girls were old enough that I didn't need to hire a babysitter anymore, and I would look forward to getting out and socializing with my friends.

We would typically go to Sea Dog Pub then to Barnaby's Nightclub. Our crowd of people—friends we had known for years—would be at those same places. It was always fun to walk in and see who was there. Talking, drinking, and doing a little flirting and dancing was my escape. Most of the time, I was with close girlfriends and we would hit the dance floor as soon as we got there and not leave it until it was time to go home. I loved the loud dance music and the people. The energy in a dance club is always great for me.

As my mediumship developed, I realized that I was being pushed to go talk to people, and I always got very accurate messages when I was out. Whether it was from the energy of the people or the music or the combination of the two, I was an awesome medium in those situations.

One night, an attractive man walked into Barnaby's, and I couldn't take my eyes off of him—I was totally drawn to him. I'm not a shy person, and I'm even less inhibited with a cocktail in my body as liquid courage, so I approached him. As I stood near him, I felt, *Oh, it's not because he is attractive.* I realized that I was going to give him a message.

I stepped up to him and said, "Hi, I'm Melissa. I know this will sound strange, but I'm a medium and I'm getting messages for you. Do you mind if I tell you?"

He gave me a skeptical look. I'm not sure if he just didn't want to tell me no or if he was actually curious about what I was going to tell him. Keep in mind, this was way before all the shows that are out today were on TV. John Edwards' "Crossing Over" and Sylvia Brown's appearances on a few talk shows were really the only programs with popular mediums at the time.

I started speaking. "They are telling me that your marriage isn't a bad marriage." He wasn't wearing a wedding ring—I had looked when he came in. "But it isn't all that you hoped it would be. They are saying that you need to make a decision soon. They are showing me that you are interested in another woman who has long brown hair and is a little smaller than me. I don't know if she works in an office, but I'm seeing the place where I used to go get my dependent military ID."

He shrugged and said, "I really don't know what you're talking about."

I continued, undaunted by his skepticism, "You have a very young daughter that has an artistic gift, and if you encourage this, she could be famous for her art someday."

He looked at me and said, "My daughter is 7."

I gave him a few more messages and left him with, "I just give what I get." I left him, thinking, *That was a waste of time.* I felt very strongly about what I was getting, but if he didn't accept it, then oh well.

I went back to the dance floor, and about five minutes later, I felt a tug on my sleeve. I turned, and it was the guy from before.

He said, "Can I talk to you for a minute?" I nodded and followed him off the dance floor. He said, "I don't know how you do what you just did, but you have a true gift. My marriage is exactly how you described. I am interested in another woman who has long brown hair. She is 5-foot-5 and 120 lb."

I said, "I'm 5-foot-6-and-a-half, and we are discussing weight, but that is a little smaller than me."

He grinned and said, "She is the wife of a friend in the military. And I have a daughter who is 2, and I think that is who you said has the artistic ability. What do I need to do to encourage her?"

I gave him some advice. I felt very validated and satisfied. I thanked him for that.

He then looked at me and said, "Can you read my friend?"

I smiled and said, "Yes, where is your friend?"

We walked to the back of the room, and he introduced me to his friend who said, "Wow, he told me what you said to him. What do you get for me?"

I immediately felt a strong message. "I'm hearing if you are already questioning something now, don't do it. I feel like you are making a big decision, but you're not sure it is right for you." He looked to his friends with a shocked face. I went on with a few more messages, and then I was done.

Afterwards, his friend said to me, "He's supposed to be getting married but was just talking to us about whether he should go through with it or not."

Another night, I was dancing with a guy from out of state. I looked at him and said, "Every time I look at you, I see a red Corvette." He looked surprised. I explained that I was a medium.

He said, "What else do you see?"

I said, "The car is pulling into a circular driveway. There's a big building and something about planes."

He smiled and said, "I do drive a red Corvette. I work at an airport, and it is a circular drive up to the building I work in."

There were no other messages. Maybe that was psychic rather than mediumship; I'm not sure. Maybe it was to make him question his beliefs. I believe there was a reason, but I am just not privy to what it was.

Another time I was with a friend who was also very spiritual and took classes with me. We were at Sea Dog when I felt compelled to go talk to a guy who was standing alone. It felt as if there was a hand on my back, trying to move me towards him. I said to my friend, "I have to go say something to that guy."

He grimaced and said, "I don't know how you dare do that."

I said, "I have tried not to before, and I get so uncomfortable that I have to go do it to feel better." He watched as I went over to the guy. I said one sentence to him that I don't remember now.

The guy grinned and said, "Thank you, I really needed to hear that." Then I was done.

I've learned to trust that they won't make me go talk to someone who will call me a freak and make a scene. That was my fear when I first started to approach people. I do believe they put me in places and at certain times to help people.

One night I was out with friends, and I did five readings as soon as I walked through the door. Finally, an hour later, I was just ordering my first glass of wine when a co-worker approached and said, "Melissa, this is my friend. You need to do a reading for her."

I was starting to feel a little irritated that I hadn't even talked to my friends or had a drink yet when I heard the woman say, "But I'm scared."

All of a sudden I had this feeling like "you know better, little girl," and I turned around and said, "Love is energy and that never dies. You know that, and someone is saying, 'Don't worry, the grass is greener on the other side.'"

She immediately burst into tears. I was starting to feel bad, wondering if I had sounded annoyed or something. She regained her composure and said, "That is what my dad said on his death bed before he passed: 'Don't worry about me. I know the grass is greener on the other side.'" She smiled at me through tears. She asked if she could meet with me at another time for a reading. I felt truly blessed to have been their tool that night. I believe I helped a lot of people, and I did finally get my glass of wine.

Over the years, there have been many random readings while I've been out. I don't remember most of what I say to people, and sometimes I do not remember them at all. People will come up to me like we are best buddies and give me a hug and say, "Melissa, it is so good to see you!"

If I don't recognize them, I'll act just as happy to see them and say, "Hey you... How are you?"

The messages aren't for me, and for as long as I've been doing this, it would be impossible to remember them all. I don't retain them unless there was something significant or very evidential that even surprises me. I am more likely to remember the evidential ones that I did in the very beginning because they were what helped me and gave me the confidence to do what I do now. I am grateful for those.

Souls' Decision

Bangor, Maine

As I left the local dance club one night at 1 a.m., I said good-bye to my friends. We always have a great time. I love to dance. The energy of the loud music and the people dancing is always a charge for me.

As I unlocked my car to get in, I realized that my phone was ringing. I look at the caller ID and was surprised to see my dad's cell phone number. I immediately answered—something was wrong.

My dad's voice sounded worried as he said, "I wanted to let you know we brought your mother to the emergency room. We think she is having a stroke."

"Which hospital, Dad?" I asked.

He replied, "St. Joe's."

I said, "I'm on my way. Be there in 10 minutes." I hung up and "checked in" with my guides.

I heard, *It's too soon to tell. It could go either way.*

Worried, I arrived at the hospital. My dad was waiting. I went over to hug him and asked how she was doing.

He replied, "We are not sure yet." She was still being examined.

My mom's brother, Bert, was visiting from Washington State. Her sister, Sandra, lived locally. It was typical for them to go to my parents' house and the four of them would play cards until very late into the night (or maybe I should say early morning). That was what was happening when my mom started to not make sense. She got up and went to the living room and sat down.

My dad said, "I'm calling an ambulance." My mom refused to let him, not realizing the seriousness of the situation. My dad said, "Then we are headed to the hospital right now." I believe he had to threaten to pick her up and put her in the car. My mom hated hospitals.

Her blood pressure was dangerously high. They determined at the hospital that she had a bleed in her brain.

While we were waiting, I went to try to reach my brothers and sisters. My dad had tried them, but since it was the middle of the night, he'd had no luck. We were concerned that Mom might not survive.

The doctor came out and said they needed to do a surgery to stop the bleeding. He wasn't sure how extensive the damage was and wouldn't know until they operated. He allowed us to go see her while they were preparing for the surgery. She was sedated and asleep. My dad went over to her and kissed her on the head. My heart broke seeing her like that, and if I was upset, Dad had to be 10 times worse.

They had a love that everyone dreams of having. They are each other's best friend and have an amazing, loving relationship. They are the couple that always holds hands. My mom sits in the middle of the seat in the truck beside my dad. They kiss three times when leaving or greeting each other. I am so blessed to have this love as an example.

When they were younger, before they were married, my dad was in the Navy. They tell a story of how, once when he was out on the ship going into a foreign port, he sent my mom a letter and asked if it was okay to have her name tattooed on his arm. She says she wrote back and said no. He wrote back to her and said, "Too late." We all smile at this. At the time that my mom was waiting for surgery, they had been happily together for 40 plus years and as of this writing, they have been married for 55 years.

When Dad was stationed in Virginia, he would hitchhike home most weekends to see her. It's a 16-hour drive on a good day. He would get picked up by people wanting to help out a service man. He would get in the car and fall asleep. It had to have been less scary back in the early 1960s, but I'm sure there were still risks. My dad never worried about anything… that is until that night.

I couldn't even imagine one of my parents without the other. My dad has always been the most easy-going, loving, and supportive person I have ever known. I am and always will be a daddy's girl. I have stated many times, "My dad is the only perfect man God ever created, with the possible exception of Jesus."

Seeing my mother lying there, I was so upset. I went to put my hands on her and do some spiritual healing/reiki and heard, *Hands off. You cannot do that until she decides what she is going to do.*

I was so confused. How could my mom decide anything? Then it was explained.

The soul makes the decision. Depending on how extensive the damage is, she may decide to come home. I felt more than heard that my mother would not want to stay and be a burden on any of us. If her quality of life wasn't going to be good, she wouldn't want to stay. I couldn't share this. I kept it to myself.

The rest of the family started showing up. The waiting room was pretty much full of mostly my family. We are blessed to be close to each other.

We are the family that still gets together every Sunday. It is such a comfort when facing this type of situation.

My mom came out of her surgery. The doctors knew there was some brain damage but weren't sure how much. It was really a wait-and-see game. She finally woke up in the afternoon. I felt a sense of relief. I truly felt that if she was going to "go home," she wouldn't have woken up after her surgery.

I went home and finally slept after being up almost 40 hours straight. As I dozed off, I felt like everything was going to be okay.

It was a long hospital stay and many days of occupational therapy. She had to relearn so much. She had many challenges, but she is strong and I am so proud of her.

A few years later, I had another experience where similar information came to me.

My dad had had knee surgery on both his knees. He wanted them both done at the same time so he wouldn't have to worry about being away from my mom twice. After the surgery, he was sent to Bangor Nursing and Rehab to heal.

One evening while I was visiting my dad, I left his room to find the ladies room. As a walked down the hallway, I saw angels standing by the doors of the rooms. As I passed, I glanced in and saw very old and frail bodies. It seemed like some of them were barely alive. I didn't understand why the angels didn't take them.

My thoughts were heard, and in response I heard, *We don't take them. We guide them to the other side when they decide they are ready to go, or when the body gives out.*

I thought, *Why do they stay?*

I heard, *Some still have unfinished business—something they want to say to someone or someone they want to see before they go. Others have a fear; they worry about judgment and are afraid they were not good enough to get into heaven.*

I thought, *How sad.* I wish they could know what I know.

There is no judgment from God or angels; they are unconditional love—only loving and supporting us. We are the ones who judge ourselves when we get home. We set certain expectations of ourselves as we choose our paths that we experience here in the physical world. We may experience disappointment if we didn't handle something as well as we expected, for example. When we get to the other side, we have understanding of why everything happens the way it does while we are here. We understand why there were challenges and difficult situations. We keep the joys with us. We are able to see our blessings so clearly from there. Then, we return with determination to have even more challenges because we know the only true way to learn something is to experience it. We grow as souls—we grow compassion and understanding, and we work our way towards becoming unconditionally loving beings.

But They Aren't Dead

Bangor, Maine

It had been a few years since I began working with Spirit. I was hearing and seeing clearly. I loved doing group readings. Group readings are typically held at someone's house or place of business and they are typically gallery-style readings. The energy is almost always very high in a group setting. Something happened one evening that I couldn't explain.

I was reading this woman and heard, *I'm her grandfather.* I saw a man about 5-foot-8 with white hair and a round face. He had a big smile.

I told this woman, "I have your grandfather."

She informed me that her grandfather was still living.

I asked the spirit again, *Who are you?*

The reply was: *I'm her grandfather.*

I said to her, "He says he is your grandfather." I described him.

She said, "Sounds like him, but he's still alive."

I was puzzled but asked the spirit to clarify again.

I heard, *I'm her grandfather.* Then I felt like this man was very loving and kind of a tease with a great sense of humor.

She said, "The physical description and personality sounds exactly like my grandfather, but he's still here." We continued with the reading, but I was very confused by the whole thing.

Months went by. One night, I woke up at about 2 a.m. and heard my older brother, Roy, talking to me. If I had kept my eyes closed, I would have sworn that he was standing right by my bed. My brother was not physically there, nor was he a spirit. He is alive and well still. My brother's spirit told me about something that was going on with his wife's health—there was a concern. I asked this energy to remind me in the morning so I wouldn't forget to tell my brother. I often wake with very vivid dreams but forget them by morning, and this felt important so I asked for the reminder.

The next day on my lunch break I called my brother. He said, "Hello" in our typical drawn out kind of way.

I said, "Hi, you came to talk to me last night." Fortunately, at this point my brother has been witness to quite a few of my oddities and was very open to hearing me out.

He responded with: "What did I say to you?"

I proceeded to tell him about what I was feeling and hearing from him. He threw out a few possibilities to which I responded, "I don't think that is what you were trying to tell me." None of his suggestions of possibilities felt right.

He said, "I have no idea, but I'll talk to Tracey about it later."

I felt happy and relieved that he was open to talking to her about this—I really was concerned for her.

A week or so went by and my whole family was getting together at a local restaurant. Tracey came over to me and said, "Roy told me about what you heard about me. I know exactly what it is, and I have seen a doctor about it." I felt validated and relieved.

Later, the reading with the woman came to mind. I started wondering about our higher selves. I do believe a part of us stays on Spirit side. Why wouldn't I be able to hear them? They are energy like any other spirit. Then I thought about all the readings I have done and wondered if they were all dead or if I was getting energies of people still living. *Is that why sometimes people cannot place who I am talking about in a reading?* From then, I heard from people that I know are still living. I hear them as if I am hearing a physical person speak. It is their voice and I feel them as if they are here.

I have also had a few people tell me that I visit them at night. It has happened several times to one friend in particular. He has said, "You were here—it wasn't a dream. You were right by my bed." Of course, he is a medium too.

Gram F

Bangor, Maine

My grandmother Flewelling—my dad's mom—was a wonderful woman. She was Irish and had a dry, sarcastic sense of humor. I, to this day, giggle at things she would say. For instance, she would tell her dog that he was the smartest kid she ever had even with my dad sitting in the room. Or she'd describe how, when her boys were babies and a woman approached the baby carriage and say, "Oh, what is it?" she always wanted to say, "It's a baby, you damn fool." But I'm sure she smiled politely and answered, "It's a boy."

She was "39 years old" the entire time I knew her, even though she was on this Earth plane for over 80 years. After my dad turned 40, she would say, "I'm the only woman in town that has kids older than me." She feigned despair.

During one of my last really good visits with my grandmother, my kids were teasing me about only being 29 years old when I was in my late 30s (obviously I came by lying about my age honestly). My gram piped up. "She can't be any older, I'm only 39," she said with as much conviction as she had 40 years earlier.

She was very loving and supportive. She was an excellent cook, and Sunday lunches were almost always at her house. She was very proud of being Irish and taught us to have pride in our family. She grew up on Cranberry Island just off Bar Harbor. She told stories about living on the island when she was a kid. They mostly centered on the dogs that her family kept during the winter for the people who had summer homes. She loved animals more than people, especially dogs. She would train them to wave goodbye and say "go out," and she even taught one to meow like a cat.

We both loved to read. We would pass books back and forth. It started when I was in high school. I remember her reading the Harlequin Silhouette books. Since I was only in high school, she said, "I'm not sure if you should read these or not—they are a little spicy."

I grinned and said, "It's fine." Then I put those on top of the pile.

I always had my face in a book. My gram, her sister, and I would write our initials in the books so we would know who had read which book and who they needed to be passed to next. We read hundreds of books.

When I got married and moved to Kentucky, Gram wrote me letters. I used to look forward to those letters from her. When I was pregnant, I was very sick. She would encourage me to tell my doctor stating, "The squeaky wheel gets the grease."

She was diagnosed with Alzheimer's after my grandfather passed. It progressed rapidly and it wasn't long before she had to be placed in a nursing home. I was working two jobs and had the kids so I didn't get to go visit her as often as I would have liked. She always knew who I was. She would repeat the stories about the dogs they took care of when she was younger. There was one story about her father trying to take a dog back to the owners, but he was sneaky and got back on the boat and hid to go back to the island.

There was another story about how every year in the fall her mom would send her into the living room to go get her a book and my unsuspecting grandmother would be surprised to see the dog waiting excitedly to see her. She would talk about how the dog would usually get excited to see them come home from school, but on the first day back with them, he'd wait quietly in the living room. She would say, "And that dog was in on the surprise because he stayed so quiet until Mother sent me into the living room for something." The memory lit up her face. She repeated that story very often as the Alzheimer's took control. I have often wondered what my favorite memories are that my mind would repeat if that happens to me.

Years went by and I got a call from my dad. "Gram isn't doing well. She has pneumonia, and they don't think she will survive much longer. If you want to, you should go see her soon."

My sister and I went to visit her. She was propped up a bit in the bed. As she breathed out, she made an "ouch" sound. I went to sit on the edge of the bed and my sister sat on the opposite side. We held her hands. It was so awful to see her like that; my heart was breaking. She looked like she was suffering. I focused and channeled as much healing energy into her as I could.

This only went on for a couple minutes when all of a sudden, her eyes opened and she looked right at me very lucidly and said, "I'm okay." Then she went right back to breathing difficultly with her eyes closed.

I looked at my sister, shocked, and said, "Did you hear that?"

She said, "Yes. She said, 'I'm okay.'"

I truly felt that Gram's soul wasn't experiencing the pain of her body shutting down. I believe she was in and out during the last day or two. I believe she popped back into her body to comfort me and my sister during this time—she didn't want us to worry about what we were seeing.

A while after she passed, I heard her. She has come to me many times and through other mediums with messages for me. A few years after she had passed, my cat, Sassy, was hit by a car. I was so upset. We took her to the emergency vet. She couldn't move her back legs. The x-ray was inconclusive as to whether her spine was broken or not. There was only about a 10 percent chance that she would walk again. This was a Saturday night, if we waited until Monday to see, it was going to cost about $800. I didn't have the money, but I loved this cat so much. I asked to see her so I could decide. The vet walked me back to where they had her in a cage. They opened the cage and she dragged herself over to me. I started sobbing, not knowing what to do. I felt like I shouldn't let her suffer but it was so hard thinking about ending her life.

Then, loud and clear, I heard my grandmother's voice. *Melissa Jean, you do the right thing and put this cat down.*

I knew she was serious because she used my middle name. She used to say, "That's one thing we can do for animals that we cannot do for humans. When there's no more quality of life, we can put them down and end their suffering." The fact that she loved animals so much, I knew at this point there was no hope. As difficult as it was, I knew putting Sassy down was the right thing to do.

I am so grateful that Gram was there when I needed her, both when she was here physically and now in spirit form. I have so many great memories and so much love for my grandmother. I'm sure she is happy about me writing this book. I know now that she knew how much she meant to me.

Divine Timing

Etna, Maine

Gram Bryer, my mother's mother, was the kind of grandmother you think of when you think of the word 'grandmother.' She was loving, supportive, fun, and kind. She was a wonderful cook, and I have so many memories of our large family gatherings on Sundays with my aunt, uncle, and cousins.

My Grampa Bryer loved us grandkids. He liked to tease us kids. We would be watching TV and feel a tap on our shoulder and look around at him, and he would act like it hadn't been him. I remember we'd scratch his back for him and he would give us quarters. He would take us into his garden and peel the red off the radishes with a jack knife so they wouldn't be hot to taste.

Looking back at that time, when we were young, I have very happy memories of spending Saturday nights at their house while my parents went out dancing. My sister and I would race into their house to Gram's chair, and we would argue who got to sit beside her. We would have ice cream and watch Lawrence Welk and "Hee Haw."

My grandfather passed when I was 13. Gram called our house looking for my parents who were out. My sister had answered the phone and said Gram was upset. I could feel that something was seriously wrong. My stomach hurt and I started vomiting. When my parents got home, they told us the news. I remember crying and going to bed.

The next day as I waited for the bus to go to school, I started crying again. My dad hugged me and said in his very gentle tone, "You don't have to go to school today." I went in the living room, lay down on the couch, and watched TV. After everyone went to school or work, I fell asleep. I dreamt of my grandfather. When I awoke, I heard his voice say, *Don't worry, I'm okay.*

I felt better, less sad. I shrugged it off as part of the dream. Now I know that it was probably the first time I heard a spirit that I can remember. It was amazing how the grief left me after that. I didn't have that devastating sadness anymore.

Gram lived another 20 or more years after he passed. She loved to go out with friends to play Bingo. She was very lucky and won often. She stayed very active.

One day, we were celebrating my daughter Joelle's birthday, and most of the family was there. Gram came with my parents. She was going to be staying the night at their house. She still lived alone at 88. We had a great time as always when the family gets together.

The next morning, I was going to church. Joelle like to spend time at my parents' house while I was gone, so I decided that I would drop her off there on my way. That particular morning, I left my house early, hoping my dad could help me switch out the wiper blades on my car. I had purchased new ones and had tried several times but couldn't get the old ones off.

I arrived at my parents' in plenty of time and my dad came out to help with the wipers. After a couple minutes, mom came running outside, panic evident on her face. She said, "There's something wrong with mom!"

We ran inside. Dad called 911. I sat by Gram and channeled healing into her. I talked to her and said, "You're going to be fine." It seemed as if she was having a stroke. I held her hand and said some silent prayers. I was calm and collected. I think the angels help me with that. I needed to be calm for Gram. My mom was justifiably upset, and my dad was comforting her. The ambulance came and took to Gram to the hospital. My parents followed in their car.

We weren't sure what medications my Gram was taking so I went to her house and got her prescription bottles. When I got to the hospital, it was confirmed that it had been a stroke and that it didn't look like she would survive it. I called my brothers and sisters and told them what was going on. My younger brother lived in New Hampshire and said he would be up as soon as he could.

By the time they had put her in a room, all of the family but my younger brother had arrived. I sat holding her hand and sending healing into her. I don't believe she was still in her body, but I talked to her anyway. My younger brother arrived, and she passed about 15 minutes later. I swear her body just stayed alive until he could say his goodbyes.

I left the hospital shortly after. I finally cried on the way home. But I had the thought, *What a way to go—with all your loved ones around you.* Most of the family had seen her the night before at my house and great memories of her laughing and smiling.

Two days later, it was raining. I tried one more time to put the new wipers on. This time, they popped right off easily. I installed the new ones and thought, *Wow, did that all happen so I would be there when my family needed me? Divine timing.* I normally would not have been at my parents' house at that time of morning. If I hadn't needed help with the wipers, I would not have been there early.

At her funeral, I heard my Gram say, *Tell them when they think of me, I'll be there.*

At that time, I was still very much in the closet about my abilities. I said it to some people, but did not say "Gram said..." I think she understands.

She has come through many times and I am grateful to still maintain the connection with her beautiful soul.

Survivor's Guilt

2006
Bangor, Maine

~~~~

I had gotten to the point where I was booking readings and doing them at my house on Essex Street in Bangor. On this particular day, three young ladies—all of whom I'm guessing were in their early to mid-20s—arrived at my house for readings.

When I do readings, I like to just spill everything I get, then leave a few minutes to allow the person to ask a question. The instructions are something like this every time I do a reading whether it's in a group setting or a single, private reading: "I like to just say what I'm getting. I prefer if you do not talk during. If you don't understand what I am saying, then feel free to say that you don't understand, and I'll see if I can get more information. If you do understand what I'm saying, and I'm going into more detail then feel free to say 'I understand,' and I'll move on. I will give you a chance to ask questions or give validation at the end. I believe that if you start giving me feedback during, one of two things are likely to happen—either later you will question what you said and if it led me to say what I said next, or you will say something evidential that I was just about to say and you won't believe me when I say that I was just going to say that. I need you to know that what I'm getting it is coming from Spirit, and you are not feeding me information. Don't feed the medium." Then I smile at my own joke.

The first young lady nodded her head as I was talking, and I knew she understood the messages coming through. The second lady was a little less obvious about what she was thinking, but did validate when I was done. Both validated and I felt okay about how it went.

I truly believe that if you come for entertainment, they will entertain you but not give you the "holy crap, you're freaking me out" kind of moments. However, if you are in need, you're grieving, or you need to know that you're not alone or need to know your loved one in Spirit is in a good place, that is when even I can get impressed with the detail of what Spirit gives me. I do believe that they do not give proof beyond reasonable doubt most of the time. We are not meant to know the inner workings of the spiritual realm until we return back to our energetic state.

I will never forget the third woman. As soon as I started her reading, I immediately got a young man. He died in his 20s. I relayed this information and said, "I believe it was a motorcycle accident—definitely accident." She sat with a blank look on her face.

I said, "He is saying he loves you. He's talking about whiskey. Whiskey is significant with him." A tear trickled down her face.

I continued: "He's saying he never danced with you."

She broke my rule and, through tears, said, "That is my fiancé who died, and when he drank whiskey and would get mean, he never danced with me even if he was drunk. Drunk or sober, it didn't matter, he would not dance with me."

I continued, "He is saying he loves you and wants you to be happy and move on. It's okay to be happy." My heart broke for her as more tears rolled down her face and I thought, *How sad to lose someone you love at such a young age.*

Then he said, *She will be with someone that treats her like she should be treated and that will love her better than I did.*

I relayed that information. More tears fell. I felt his love for her and could feel that he just wanted her to be happy and know it was okay to move on. I explained that to her. I said, "He wants you to live a happy life and know that he is okay with you moving on. He wants that for you. He is saying you will be with someone who will dance with you and treat you right." Then I start hearing the song "I Wear My Sunglasses at Night" by Corey Hart in my head. I looked at her kind of puzzled and said, "Now I'm hearing the song 'I Wear My Sunglasses at Night.'" I sang a little bit of it.

She looked shocked and said, "My current boyfriend has that song for a ringtone on his phone, and I make fun of him all the time for it."

We finished the reading, and I really felt that her deceased fiancé had come through and had given her what she needed. She was feeling guilty about moving on and living a happy life because she didn't know how she could be happy when he was dead. I explained to her that our loved ones on the other side have a clear picture of why everything happened in their life here. The best thing we can do for those who have passed is to wish them well and be happy that they are back "home." We need to continue here, and if we are happy, they will be happy for us. It is painful for them to watch us struggle.

I really felt like when she left that she felt lighter—that she knew it was okay to just be happy. That is when I knew that what I do is truly a gift.

Angel Flight

2010
Boston, Massachusetts

In September 2010, I was dating a police officer named Dan, who was also a pilot. He flew for Angel Flight, a program that consists of pilots who volunteer to fly cancer patients to Boston from Bangor for treatments. He was scheduled to take a patient to Boston and asked me to go along.

He said, "We can spend the day in Boston while she has her treatments." I jumped at the chance. Not only did I enjoy time with Dan and love Boston, I loved to fly. I was very excited to go. A day or two later, he called back and said, "The patient's mom is going, so I'm sorry—it will be too much weight in the plane so I can't take you this time." I was disappointed but I completely understood.

The next day, we talked on the phone again. Dan said, "Melissa, I was thinking. If I only fill the plane half-full of fuel—plenty enough to get us to Boston—I can refuel there and that would allow for more weight in the plane. I really want to take you to Boston."

I was so excited and said, "Yes, I'd love to go."

The day arrived and it was a beautiful fall day. Dan picked me up at my house, and we drove to the General Aviation building at the airport. We arrived at the airport about 10 minutes later. Before Dan left to make his preparations for the plane, I handed him a gift. It was an angel ornament to hang in the plane. He smiled and thanked me with a hug and kiss. He was always so kind to me, I wanted to give him something to show him that I cared, and the silver angel ornament seemed so appropriate.

We met the patient and her mother, then we all got in the plane and prepared for takeoff. I was excited, but I was feeling the struggle of the patient. I checked in with my guides and angels about offering to do some healing on her while we flew.

I had my reiki 3 certification but prefer to call it "spiritual healing," mostly because that was what I was doing before taking reiki classes. I felt my hands warm and tingle. Dan knew that I was a medium and was supportive. Once we were in the air, I knew we had a little while before arriving in Boston. I turned around to the patient and her mother and explained that I was a medium and did spiritual healing. I asked if I could do a reading and healing work. I explained to them a little about my history and that my hands were getting hot already from the energy that was starting to flow through me. They agreed.

I placed my hands on her, and the energy flowing warmed me. I gave her some messages of hope. She had been battling cancer for quite a long time. Once I was done, she thanked me, and I felt good about what had happened between us. I turned back around and enjoyed the rest of the flight to Boston. Dan played music in our headphones and it was so relaxing with the sun shining in the cabin of the plane.

We arrived in Boston. The patient and her mother were taken to the treatment center, and Dan and I headed out to explore Boston. I had been to Boston many times and love everything the city has to offer. It was a lovely sunny day, and we only needed light jackets as we walked through the streets.

We decided to go the aquarium; I hadn't been in there in many years. We had a great time strolling through the building and seeing the penguins, fish, and other types of ocean creatures. Dan was a very easy-going and fun guy to spend time with doing anything. We spent an hour or so in the aquarium and decided to go to lunch at Quincy Hall. There were so many choices, but we settled on lunch at Cheers. We enjoyed an adult beverage while we ate. We sat outside and took our time. I was really having a wonderful day. We walked around a bit after lunch until we received the call that the treatments were done, and it was time to head back to the airport.

We arrived back at the airport and assisted the patient and her mom into the plane. She was exhausted and was very quiet. I said a quick silent prayer that she would heal quickly. We climbed in and prepared for takeoff.

Just as Dan started the engine, I had a horrible, gut-wrenching feeling—something was wrong. I physically felt pain in my abdomen with the energy of the warning. I quickly checked in with my guides and angels and heard, *Melissa, don't worry. You will be fine.*

I didn't say anything to Dan. We started to roll towards the runway and an airport agent stopped us. Dan opened the window, and I heard the gentleman say, "You have a slack tire. We need you to fill it up before we allow you to take off."

Dan seemed to think that they were being overly cautious because it was barely slack. I thought that maybe that was what was wrong. Dan pulled over and filled the tire up. We started to roll again, and again I had a painful feeling in my belly. *Something is very wrong.* I looked at Dan and he seemed fine.

I asked in my head again, *What is wrong? Do I need to stop this flight?*

I heard, Melissa, you will all be fine, don't worry. I didn't say anything to Dan. I had to trust.

I felt so nervous. I'm not a nervous person, but I knew something was wrong, and as much as I trusted that we would be fine, I couldn't shake the feeling. As we took off I could see very dark clouds behind us. It looked like a serious thunderstorm coming in. I wondered is that what was making me nervous.

Melissa, you are fine, was heard in my head again.

We were a few minutes into the flight, and Dan put on some music in the headphones. Music always calms me. Then the most incredible thing happened—the clouds broke and the most beautiful sunset appeared. The sun shone golden and the clouds around a deep red and gold. The interior of the plane even appeared pinkish. I had the most peaceful feeling as if I were among the divine. I felt blessed and was grateful. I took many photos and videos with a little flip-cam.

We arrived back in Bangor after what I had thought was an uneventful flight. We helped the patient back to her car, and her mother drove them away.

Dan looked at me and said, "We need to check out the plane."

I said, "Why, what is wrong?"

He explained that after takeoff, at about 600 feet, the plane had backfired. He said, "I'm surprised you didn't hear it. We lost power but continued to climb, so I kept going but I kept an eye on all the airports on the way back thinking we would have to make an emergency landing."

I looked at him with big eyes and said, "I knew something was wrong, but 'they' said don't worry, so I didn't say anything."

We walked back to the plane. He opened the hood over the engine and looked in. He said, "That's what it was," as he pointed to a hole in the exhaust. "We are lucky that hole in the exhaust wasn't closer to the gas line."

We both counted our blessings and silently sent up thanks for whoever had kept us safe. Dan said, "I'll have to have a mechanic look at it, but I think this plane is done." I felt sad. It was too bad that had happened when he used the plane for such good things as Angel Flights.

Dan took me home. It was getting late. I went into my house and got ready for bed, thinking over the day's events and feeling like my "ability" was a true blessing. I hesitate to call it a gift. To me, that implies that I was chosen or special when I really feel that I'm sensitive and worked to hone my connection with spiritual and angelic realms.

I woke up later than usual the next morning. I got up and jumped in the shower, and then I started getting ready for my day. I went into the kitchen to grab something to eat and my phone rang. It was Dan.

"Good morning," I said with a smile.

He said, "Melissa, I am so glad that you and your angels were with us yesterday." There was an intensity in his voice indicating there was more to the story.

I said, "Why are you saying that now?"

He said that the plane mechanic had looked at the plane. "Melissa, he insists that there is no way my plane made it from Boston to Bangor with this much damage. The mechanic said that the magneto had exploded, and there were shards of metal all through the engine. He insists that this plane could not have flown from Boston to Bangor," he repeated. "Your angels kept us flying."

I was dumbfounded, but with every experience that I'd had to this point, I truly believed him. This was not the first or last time the angels intervened to keep me alive. Whatever my purpose, "they" are not done with me yet.

Dan told me how expensive it was going to be to repair, and I could hear the discouraged tone loud and clear. I wished I had the money to help him out, but I was living paycheck to paycheck.

A week or so later, Dan called me and said that he had found a benefactor who generously donated money to cover the costs of the repair to the plane. We were so happy and thankful. The angels were taking care of everything.

Jesus

2006-2007
Carmel, Maine

⌁

One night when I was deep in meditation, I saw Jesus. I immediately thought, *Why am I seeing Jesus?* I was not an overly religious person. However, this event made me question and rethink my beliefs.

I heard Jesus talking to me. He explained that Mandi, my sister-in-law's daughter, was having a boy and that this baby was special and needed to be here. He explained that there were problems with the pregnancy, but we could help. He would channel through me for a healing. Even as I write this, reliving it, I am still in awe. I cried as this divine energy connected with me.

I spoke with Tracey, my sister-in-law, the next day. I explained that I was getting that I needed to do a healing with Mandi. I was near tears as I explained. The emotion of connecting with Jesus's energy was still with me. For weeks, every time I thought about it or mentioned it to the few people I told, I would cry. Tracey did mention that Mandi was having complications with her pregnancy. At this point, they hadn't been told that it was a boy.

Tracey, my sister Mindy, Mandi, and I planned a day to go shopping. We went to southern Maine to some outlet malls. We had a good day. When we got back to my sister's house where we met, I said, "Mandi, is it okay for me to do the healing now?"

She said, "I guess so." She was tired.

I moved to where I could put my hands on her lower back. I put my hands on her and visualized reaching up and connecting. I felt this energy flow through me and my hands started to intensely tingle and get hot. I broke out in a sweat. Mandi said, "Wow, I feel like you just put a heating pad on my back." I allowed the energy to flow for a few minutes, then felt that I was done.

I thanked her for being open to letting me do it. I was amazed by what had happened, but my logical mind always questioned things and gave me doubts. I always want signs for validation—big blinking neon signs. And that is what I got.

A couple weeks went by, and we did get confirmation that Mandi was having a boy. Her issues were getting better.

I went to my parents' house one Sunday not long after. When I walked in, Tracey said, "Did Mandi call you?"

I replied, "No, why?"

She said, "The weirdest thing happened to her when she was shopping at Wal-Mart. An old woman walked up to her and touched her on the arm and looked at her belly and said, 'That baby boy has been blessed by Jesus.'"

I was shocked and had to blink back tears.

I started taking a class at the church with the then-president, Sandy Scott. She was leading the class and asked about experiences we have had. I talked about my Jesus experience and expressed doubt.

"Why would Jesus talk to me?" I asked.

She looked at me like that was the stupidest question she had ever heard and replied, "Because you can hear him Melissa."

I thought, *Oh, there is that.*

About a month went by and I was going to gallery readings at the Harrison D. Barrett Memorial Spiritualist Church in Bangor. Years later, I became a member and now serve as the president on the board. On the second Friday of every month, we have mediums do gallery-style readings. All day that day, I heard, *Bonnie Lee is going to say something important, pay attention.* I kept hearing it over and over throughout the day. I didn't even know if Bonnie Lee was the scheduled medium.

My friend and I got to church, and sure enough, Bonnie Lee Gibson and her husband Ernie Vanden Bossche were the mediums who were serving. Ernie did an amazing job giving me a reading. I had absolutely no doubt that he had connected with my Gram Flewelling. Very evidential information came through about her. I was grateful but thought, *I thought Bonnie was supposed to do my reading?*

After my reading, Ernie said, "Bonnie, do you want to take over."

Bonnie came up from the back of the room and started giving messages to a girl right across the aisle from me. She all of a sudden stopped mid-sentence, turned to me and said, "They aren't done with you yet, I need to tell you that Jesus is with you." I couldn't stop the tears from falling. I was so grateful for more validation.

Lucas, Mandi's son, was born strong and healthy. I would watch my mom hold him after her stroke and see this peaceful bliss across her face and I believed this boy *was* special somehow.

I finally thought, *Okay, this is real.* It has always been hard for me to accept this and talk about the experience that seemed so incredible. Whether it was not feeling worthy of such a connection or whether it was too hard for my mind to comprehend that this is real, I'm not sure. Beyond all reasonable doubt, Jesus, archangels, and other divine entities are real and they can affect change and create miracles—this I know for sure. I am living proof.

Jamie

2015
Bangor, Maine

———

In 2010, I had just broken up with Chris, a boyfriend of three years. We had been living together for a year. There were a few reasons we didn't stay together, but the fact my teenage daughters were not getting along with him was the biggest reason to end it. I believe that it all happened for a reason and we were not meant to continue the path we were on.

After he moved out, my friend Jamie moved in with her son, Coby. She had been through a break-up, and this was a great situation for us all. It was inexpensive for her, and it helped me out having someone pay half of my mortgage. We had met through Chris and loved each other immediately.

I loved having her and Coby in the house. My girls got along great with her. We all lived busy lives, so it never seemed crowded in my house. My oldest, Kayla, was away at college in Portland, Maine and not living at home anymore, so I took her room next to Joelle's on the first floor, and Jamie and Coby had the two rooms upstairs. It all was great.

She and I would occasionally go for walks and end up at Sea Dog, a local restaurant and bar. We always ran into people we knew and would sometimes end up closing the bar. Those random unplanned nights out were the most fun.

The next morning, we would talk about the previous night's events and giggle as our memory of some of the happenings came back into clear focus. One time, after a particularly good night out (meaning over indulgence and relying on each other's memory of the events to fill in the blanks), she looked at me and said "I'm fairly certain there is a tiger in our bathroom." I laughed so hard while nodding in agreement at the reference from the movie, *The Hangover.*

Then along came Rusty, who really ruined most of my fun with her. She fell in love very hard and very fast. I met him and could see why. He was handsome and was a wonderful man. I was so happy for her, but it wasn't long before she moved about 30 minutes away from Bangor to Corinth to live with him. As happy as I was for them, I knew I would miss her.

We would make plans on occasion and get together, but the time in between seemed to get longer and longer. We both were living busy lives.

Then, tragically, she was diagnosed with breast cancer. We were all worried and scared. She had a mastectomy and reconstructive surgeries but did not do chemo or radiation or take the pills for prevention. She did a lot of research and decided that the risks of taking the medication outweighed the risk of doing nothing. I supported her decision. She had seen her uncle go through it and he hadn't survived. She had seen how sick he was with the chemo and didn't want it to be that way with her. She tried some holistic medicines and changed her diet. She eventually became cancer-free, and I was so proud of her for all the work and effort she'd put in to become healthy again.

A couple of years passed, and I received a phone call. Jamie had been to have some tests done because of some pain she had been having. I had been waiting for the call and praying for good news. I hoped it was something easy to repair and not anything serious.

Her voice was quiet on the phone as she told me that the cancer was back and in her bones. "It's incurable," she said.

"Oh honey, I'm so sorry," I said, my heart breaking for her for all she had already been through. "It so sucks ass!" I exclaimed.

She replied, "Oh my God, right?! Everyone has been saying, 'You can fight it, you're strong,' and all these encouraging things when I just want someone to say this f—ing sucks!"

I was never good with having a mouth filter. If it's in my head, it usually pops out of my mouth. But this time it was a good thing.

She and I met up for lunch soon after. We sat in her car and she explained how people were getting upset at her for not doing chemotherapy or radiation.

"They don't understand—this is incurable. If I do chemo, it is going to drastically reduce my quality of life, and it won't cure it."

I said, "James, I will support whatever decision you make. No one else has to live with the pain that you do. No one else will understand unless they have been in your shoes. I know if you die you will be pain-free, and that is your decision." Then looked at her and said, "Maybe it's easier for me to understand because I know you are going somewhere awesome when you die from all my experiences. I believe it will be up to you as to when you will go 'home,' and," I grinned at her, "I'll be able to talk to you anyway, so it doesn't matter to me," I teased.

She grinned. She leaned over and hugged me, and said, "I love you!"

I looked at her, knowing she just needed that unconditional support and said, "I love you more."

Time went on, and she fought. She ate well and continued to do holistic medicine that seemed to be helping for a while. I took her to Pat and Norm's, friends of mine who held a reiki share on Thursday nights. The energy they had, along with the help of other friends and me, was powerful. The first time, she was a little skeptical about the whole thing but quickly realized that the sensations the energy was creating in her body had to be doing something good because she felt better.

She planned her wedding to Rusty. We all were so happy that she had something beautiful to focus on. We all knew that this wasn't going to be a long love story, and it was a very emotional time.

I started going to her house fairly often to do more spiritual healing. I believe it is all about channeling divine energy and intent. As things progressed, I went out more often. I would have amazing visions, and I would describe them to her. The energy that flowed through me was incredible. She always felt guilty about me driving all the way out to see her, but I would assure her that it was just as beneficial to me to have that energy flow through me.

She had a cat named Mr. Timmets that was really not a friendly cat—at least not until I would start channeling the energy. No matter where he was in the house, he would come into the bedroom where we would do the session and climb up on Jamie or me as soon as the energy started to flow. He would purr loudly and rub up against me. When I was done channeling the energy, he would jump down. If I tried to pat him after it was done, he would either try to bite me or run away. He was done with me when the energy stopped.

When I channeled the energy, I would get messages for Jamie. Many were hopeful and beautiful, trying to help her understand the unconditional love of the energetic realm. Things would come to me that brought me peace as well. One that stands out the most was of her getting to the other side and being surrounded by white light or a bright white fog. In this vision, she had a confused look on her face that slowly changed to the most beautiful smile and an understanding look. Out of the white light, I saw a bunch of people approach her, and she was so happy to see them all. She was being welcomed home. As I described it, we both were in tears. Tears were rare when I was with her. Somehow, "they" always gave me the strength to keep it together while I was with her. Many times, I would cry on the way home to release my sadness.

She said, "I'm so glad I have you. No one else talks about me dying. They don't talk about the cancer. It's like a topic to avoid. It's almost as if we don't talk about it, it's not real."

I said, "I'm sure they are uncomfortable, and it's scary and they don't know what to say." She hugged me. I said, "We can talk about anything because nothing makes me uncomfortable, and I lack a filter." She grinned knowing firsthand the truth of that statement.

Time passed too quickly and the disease progressed. She went to a treatment center across the country in Oregon, and I didn't see her for a few weeks. She came home to Maine and looked so different. I could feel that we were nearing the end. My friend Louie and I did some healing on her together a few times. We are each other's batteries, and I felt she got an extra super charge when he was with me.

The long-dreaded phone call came. Rusty called. He had taken her to the hospital. It wouldn't be too long before they would send her home for hospice. I went to the hospital. Rusty talked to me and said, "Mel, she hasn't signed the advanced directive yet. We need her to. Can you talk to her and see if she will for you?"

She looked so sad. I went over and sat on the edge of the bed and said, "Hi, James. Honey, can you please sign the papers? It is to protect you and everyone else."

She didn't speak. A tear slid down her cheek, and my heart broke into a millions pieces. I thought, *Oh no, after all this time and talking, she is not ready to go.* I said out loud, "Okay, James. Not now, but soon okay?" She nodded.

I stayed for a little while. She fell asleep and her eyes immediately went into REM state. I heard, *We are working with her to remind her what it is like to come home. Don't worry, we will help her.*

I left to let her sleep and give her family some alone time with her. I went home and cried my eyes out all night. I was so heartbroken, knowing she wasn't ready.

The next day, I went back to the hospital. She was sitting up in the bed smiling. There was a peaceful feeling and a completely different energy coming from her—a level of acceptance, I suppose.

I fed her a popsicle and dropped a piece on her hospital johnny. I looked at her, not sure what to do as I picked it off her. "Want it or throw it out?"

She quickly responded, "Five second rule!" and opened her mouth so I could drop it in.

Her dad called and obviously was crying on the phone. "Dad," she said, "it's fine. Stop, it's going to be okay," as she looked at me and put her fist to her eyes like pretending to wipe tears and mouthed "waah" making light of the situation.

Later that day, she went home—no more hospitals. They set her up in the living room on a hospital bed. It was Monday.

I went out to see her Tuesday, and she was weaker and wasn't awake much.

On Wednesday, I went to see her, and Rusty said, "She hasn't responded to anyone yet today, just to warn you."

I said, "I'm going to do some reiki on her anyway if that's okay with you." He agreed.

I went over and sat on the side of the bed and prayed. I put my hands on her and felt the energy flow. She opened her eyes and looked at me. I smiled and said, "Hi James."

She said, "Hi," in a sweet, loving tone that was barely above a whisper.

I said, "I love you."

She said, "I love you too," as her eyes started to close. That was the last physical conversation we had.

The next day, her cousin Kim called me at work and said, "It won't be long. If you want to be here, you should come now."

I called my boss and through a broken voice said, "Jamie's cousin just called—"

He cut me off. "Melissa, go. You don't need to explain." He had been so supportive of me taking time off to be with her during treatments and leaving early to go see her.

I flew to my car and drove out to Corinth as fast as I could. I got there just after her dad drove in the driveway. I went in the house and knew I was too late. Rusty was by her bed, her family and his were all crying. I broke down. I went over and kissed her head and put my hand on Rusty trying to give him some support. My heart was breaking but more so for Rusty. Then I went to hug her mom. As I stepped back, I stood there crying just wanting to be support for the family but feeling the weight of my own grief.

Then, out of nowhere, Jamie's spirit was right in front of me. I could see her clearly.

In a sarcastic tone that we both appreciated, she said, *I'll be glad when you all stop blubbering.*

I grinned through my tears and told her mother what I had just seen and heard.

She smiled and said, "I believe that Melissa. She said that to her uncle on Tuesday when he stopped by to see her."

I had never heard her say "blubbering" before so that was great validation. We both took comfort in the fact that we knew she is okay. The body dying was just part of the process to get her home, and her spirit was out of pain and still sassy.

I am blessed that our friendship still carries on even if she isn't physically here. One night, I was upset about a guy I was dating and was lying on my bed, crying after a fight. I felt her and then saw her lying facing me on the other side of the bed. She said, *Get rid of him. You do not need this in your life*. She always had my back and always will. It was so comforting to hear her. I followed her advice.

There are so many awesome memories we had over the years, and I am truly blessed to have called her my friend.

Hydroplaning

April 2017
Near Augusta, Maine

I was so excited to get out of work and drive to southern Maine to see my daughter Joelle. She was pregnant and was going to have an ultrasound the next day to determine the sex of the baby. It was a dreary day with light rain, but it didn't dampen my mood.

As I drove the two hours south, I thought how happy I was that they moved home to Maine last fall from North Dakota. She and her fiancé, Jason, had only been back for a few months. They had lived in North Dakota for his job for over three years. It would have been so hard not being near her during this time. Two hours was way better than 36 hours.

As I drove, I thought about how excited I had been when she told me. I received the call on December 27 while I was at work. It wasn't typical for her to call me at work. She said, "Mom, I have some news."

"Oh?" I replied. "What is that?"

"I'm pregnant," she said.

I said, "Joelle, that is not funny."

Two days earlier when we all gathered at my parents' house for Christmas, my nephew Brien informed the family that his wife, Kayla, was pregnant. There was not a dry eye in the place—we were all so happy. My youngest niece was 16, so it had been a long time since there was a baby in the family. We were all ecstatic. I looked at my daughter and said, "I can't wait to be a grandmother. I wish I was having a grandbaby."

My oldest daughter, Kayla, and her husband, BJ, had been married a couple years at that point. His mother and I had been strongly hinting for grandchildren since the engagement. I love babies and couldn't wait to spoil a grandchild. I was super excited about the great niece or nephew and only hoped they could come home from Texas more.

I was in denial when Joelle told me she was pregnant because she wouldn't have been above that type of prank. I truly thought she was just messing with me.

She responded, "Mom, I really am. I took a test."

Still doubtful, I said, "Joelle, for real?" She started crying and I knew it was real. I practically screamed into the phone, "I'm going to be a Mimi!" I couldn't have been more thrilled. She was so emotional. I think me being doubtful made her think that I wasn't going to be happy. We chatted for a bit longer. I was so happy, but she made me wait to tell anyone until after they had seen the doctor.

As I continued my drive down, all I could think about was the baby and how Joelle had been so sick. The poor girl ended up being like me and had a hard time even keeping water down. She had lost weight. She was still working as a bartender and waitress at a restaurant in South Portland. I was amazed at her strength and so proud of her but worried at the same time. She was through her first trimester, and I was hoping she would get better soon.

We focused on planning a gender reveal party that would be the following Saturday. Since it was near Easter, she chose to do Easter eggs that we would put the pink or blue paper inside. When cracked, they would reveal the sex to the friends and family attending. They were hoping for a boy. I didn't care. I would be pleased with either sex.

I was about 10 minutes from Augusta, and I needed a restroom break. I was about halfway there and was making good time. Even though it was drizzling, it wasn't pooling on the roads, so I maintained the speed limit of 70 miles per hour, singing poorly but loudly with my radio.

All of a sudden, I started to hydroplane. My old 2002 VW Jetta swerved toward the ditch on the right side of the road. I thought, *I'm going to need a new car now.* I was sure that I was going to leave the road. Then my car turned, and I was sliding down the road sideways at 70 miles per hour. I remember thinking, *How is this not rolling over?*

Suddenly I was back in my lane but sliding backwards. I was looking at an oncoming tractor-trailer truck. I could see that it was trying to slow down. *This is really going to hurt.* I thought, *How am I going to get my car turned around and not leave the pavement or stop and not have the tractor-trailer crash into me?* Then my car spun again. It came to a complete stop on the edge of the road in the passing lane, tires on the edge of the payment. I was looking into a pretty deep ditch. The tractor-trailer passed me and pulled off to the right. I started my car, which had stalled, and started to back up and get myself back into a lane. Once I drove forward, the tractor-trailer truck pulled back on the road and drove away, obviously seeing that I was okay. My car was filled with green light. My whole body was shaking. I sent up an immediate thanks to the angels. I believe it was the archangel Gabriel, due to the green light in my car. I gave him an air high-five and said, "Nice maneuvering, Gabriel."

My car should not have stayed on the road. It defies all logic. I pulled into the rest area and made a video and posted it to Facebook.

My daughter saw the video and called. "Mom! Are you okay?"

I said, "Yes, I'm fine."

She said, "It's a good thing. If you died before finding out the sex of the baby, I would have been so pissed off." I laughed. It is our sense of humor.

My daughter and I watched the video again and laughed about how I looked. It was clear that, when I recorded the video, my adrenaline was still very high. "Mom," Joelle said, "I know why this happened!"

I said, "Why, Joelle?"

She replied, "So you would have another angel story to tell at church and your events."

I agreed with a smile, believing that it was possible.

Michael Gallagher

December 2018
Bangor, Maine

I met Mike Gallagher in the fall of 2004. We just clicked when we met. We were instant friends and were very attracted to one another. He was going through a divorce, and we spent time talking about that. I felt like I could help him through because at that point, I had done it twice.

We dated for a few months. He started to spend more time away from me, so I had the conversation with him about maybe he needed some time to heal from the divorce and wasn't ready for a committed relationship yet. I was really hoping to set him free and have him come back to me. That did not happen. The man broke my heart several times. To know him is to love him. We spent more time together after a break-up with a serious relationship. I was the person he could talk to and be himself. His brother told me once that Mike had said, "Mel's the only one I can really talk to."

We always remained friends. He helped me out so many times. For her 13th birthday, he bought my daughter a puppy she had been begging for. As a single mom, the financial struggle was real at times, and he loaned me money after a business I had been working for closed down. He drove me to the eye doctors when I need to have my eyes dilated. He always helped me.

A very weird and interesting thing happened when he took me to Ellsworth to the eye doctor. He was driving back. We were coming to an intersection in Holden (about 15 minutes from Bangor where I was currently living) when all of a sudden, a woman in a car came across the road in front of us as she crossed from a business on the left side of the road to one on the right. He slammed on the brakes, but I thought there was no way he would be able to stop in time. His arm reached out to brace me. Somehow he missed her. We looked at each other stunned. He said, "Mel, I do not know how we missed her. I thought we were going to T-bone her." I said, "I don't know how either but that should have been impossible to miss her."

He was very protective. He was a roofer and spent a lot of time at the gym. If I said he was in great shape it would be an understatement. One evening back when we were dating, a huge guy who was a friend of Mikey's came over to where we were sitting at a local bar. He had had way too much to drink and said to Mikey, "I just love your girlfriend." Then he lunged, reaching for me on the other side of Mikey. He knocked both bar stools over that Mike and I were sitting on. I felt Mikey's hand in my back, keeping me upright. My bar stool, Mikey's bar stool, and Mikey, with a beer in his hand, went backwards, slamming onto the floor. I couldn't believe he kept me from falling, but hit the ground hard himself without spilling one drop of his beer. I think that was the Irish in him.

Everyone who knew Mikey loved him. He was always quick with a smile or a joke. He loved everyone. One evening, we were out at our usual bar and a guy walked past him a few times, making comments. I asked Mikey what was going on. He said he didn't know.

The guy walked by again and made an aggressive comment. Mikey got up and followed him. I thought, *Uh oh, this isn't going to be good.* I thought they were going to fight. I watched from where I was sitting, and I could see Mikey talking to him. The next thing I knew, Mikey stuck his hand out for a handshake and bought the guy a beer. Then they were buddies. That is how he was—he was just a wonderful person.

He was diagnosed with ALS, Lou Gehrig's disease, in 2010. I remember the first conversation I had with him after finding out. He said, "Mel, they are saying one to three years of life left. I need to make it until Gary graduates high school." I believe Gary, his son, was 12 at the time.

I said, "Mikey, no one knows God's plan. Doctors can't be certain. If you don't give in to it, you will live a lot longer."

He told me how he said the serenity prayer every day. He quoted, "God give me the serenity to accept the things I cannot change, the courage to change the things I can, and the wisdom to know the difference."

I smiled and said, "I know that prayer." I felt like he was in a good place with it.

For the first few years, you could see a slow progression of the disease. His muscles twitched constantly in certain areas of his body that the disease was attacking. He remained positive and optimistic.

As time went on, we would see each other occasionally, but depending on who he was dating, he couldn't spend time with me due to jealousy of his girlfriends. At one point, after ending a relationship with another jealous woman, he said, "Mel, I've learned my lesson. My friends are important to me, and if a girl I'm dating doesn't like you, then that's too bad. I'm not giving up my friendship with you again." I told him I loved him and got: "Love ya too, Mel." He hugged me, and I felt that he truly meant it.

As his disease progressed, I could see that he needed more assistance. I told him that I would always be there for him. At the time, I don't think he believed me. He was already losing friends. He wasn't going out as often. He lost the movement of one of his arms and the other was very weak. He was still a smart ass. One night, I saw him out at the bar and he said, "Mel, I'd grab your ass, but my right arm doesn't work anymore and I'm not putting down my beer."

I grinned at him and said, "I can still grab yours, though," and did so. He always maintained his sense of humor.

He met Susan, a wonderful woman whom I am so blessed to call a close friend now. He moved in with her because he couldn't take care of himself any longer. He had lost the movement in both his arms and his legs were getting weaker. Susan took care of him and she didn't mind that I came to see him. I made a habit of going over every Wednesday night. She would get a little break, and I would get time with Mikey. I would stop and buy him a blizzard at Dairy Queen to feed to him. Then we would watch our paranormal shows. We loved scary movies too. "Paranormal Witness" and "Paranormal Survivor" were our faves. Being home during the day, he would watch TV all day. There was not much else he could do. He had seen the shows but would watch them with me again. He would wait for the jumpy parts and watch me. When I would jump or get startled, he would laugh at me. I would look at him and say, "The only reason you didn't jump was because you have already seen it."

We had many conversations about my spiritual beliefs. One time he asked about my belief in heaven and hell. I told him that I thought everyone's idea of heaven is different, but I knew beyond all reasonable doubt after my experiences, that it was a beautiful place to be. Then I said, "Sometimes I think hell is here on earth. Look what you are going through."

I was surprised at his answer. He said, "Mel, things could always be worse." God love him, it was true.

He had a way of putting things back into perspective for me. One time, I was upset about losing my job (the business closed) and was worried about money and possibly losing my house. He said, "Mel, at least you have your health."

That made me feel like everything I was experiencing was so insignificant compared to his ALS diagnosis. I said, "You are absolutely right. Thank you for reminding to be grateful for what I do have."

We were getting close to the end; it had been nine years since his diagnosis. That's three times longer than they expected him to last. He saw his son, Gary, graduate and join the Army, and he almost made it to his college graduation. He was so proud of his son.

One night, after he had been told that he was probably looking at a few months left, he asked me to pause the movie we were watching. He said, "Mel, I just need to tell you before I pass away that I love you, and thank you for being such a good friend to me. You mean the world to me."

I cried and told him how much I loved him and always have, and I was so blessed to have been his friend. We kissed and I hugged him, and we went back to our movie. I left with a sad but happy feeling. I'm glad we said the words before he passed.

It was almost the end. Susan was exhausted. I offered to stay the night. He had gotten so that he could barely swallow water, and everything needed to be done for him. She had been sleeping on the couch near the recliner where he stayed and had begun sleeping in. She said, "I don't get a lot of sleep down here."

I offered and stayed on a Saturday night to let her get a night's sleep. I made myself comfy on the couch, and Mikey and I stayed up late watching our shows. He dozed off, and I tried to sleep. He had to move around in his chair because he had a hard time breathing in certain positions. Every time he moved, the chair squeaked, and my head snapped to look at him. His voice was barely a whisper, so I was worried I wouldn't be able to hear him if he needed something. I got less than 15 minutes of sleep at a time. I realized that I needed to step it up more. Susan couldn't do this alone. I didn't know how she had managed thus far.

The next morning when she came downstairs, I said, "Oh my gosh, I had no idea that when you said you didn't get much sleep, you really meant not any sleep." I promised her that I would be back on Monday to stay the night again. I don't know how she did it all. She worked full time, had a special-needs son, and had her own health issues going on. She is the strongest woman I know, and if she doesn't get sainthood when she gets to the other side, I will be doing some complaining.

Monday came, and I went over. Susan had called to say that the hospice people didn't think it would be much longer. We took shifts in the night. His mom did not leave his side. She slept in the chair. She was in her 80s and was watching her 55-year-old son dying—it broke my heart.

Mikey, barely able to talk, said, "Mel, my mom snores," and he gave me a grin. He still had his humor.

At about 3 a.m., Susan was in the bedroom trying to get a little rest. He asked where she was. I told him that she was trying to get a little bit of sleep. "Do you need anything? Do you want your medicine?" I asked.

He said, "No, not until she gets up." Now, I believe he wanted to wait to have it when she was with him because he didn't want to pass without her there. Another hour went by, and he said, "Mel, I love you."

I walked to him, gave him a kiss, and said, "I love you too, so much. Is there anything I can do?"

He said no. I told him that I would be right here. He said okay. Then I said, "Mikey, when you can, come talk to me once you are over there. I know sometimes you think I'm crazy, but I will hear you and we will talk. And anytime I hear Eddie Money's 'Shakin' I know you will be with me." That was our song to dance to. I could always get him to dance if that song was played. We both loved Eddie Money.

The morning came, and Susan met with the hospice people who gave her the morphine. Mikey's brother arrived, and his best friend, Rob, was there. Mikey was ready for the morphine. Susan sat with him. I sat with Rob. As I looked towards Mikey, I could see 10 lights around him. I knew they were angels. I saw a few immediately touch him. As time progressed, I saw them connect with him one at a time.

Roby called Gary to let him know that it wouldn't be long. I knew when the last angel connected he would be done. He would have let go of his body and be in spirit form. Gary arrived minutes before the last one connected. I felt that it was the archangel Michael and could feel Mikey's feeling of humbleness at the presence of such a divine being.

He seemed to transition peacefully. I felt so blessed to have been there and to have seen what I saw and feel what I felt.

I heard Mikey the next morning. He thanked me and wanted to tell Susan that he wished he had told her how grateful he was for all the care and love she provided.

At his celebration of life service, Susan and I were setting things up. I was playing some of his favorite songs through a speaker. I felt his presence as the song was changing, and the very next song was "Shakin" by Eddie Money.

Brayson

December 2018
Bangor, Maine

⟍⟋

I met Brayson through my friend Melissa. She had messaged and asked me to come to the hospital to do some spiritual healing on her stepson, Dominick. Dominick had fallen out of the back of a truck and had fractured his skull in two places and had a serious concussion. It was scary—they were concerned about his eyes and ears having permanent damage.

Before I got to the hospital, she messaged again and said that her friend Darek's son was in the hospital too. He was 9 years old and had a brain tumor removed in the summer—he'd had radiation and was getting chemotherapy. They had had to pause his chemotherapy because he had pneumonia. She went on to say that he hadn't been able to eat in weeks, and they were concerned about his GI tract shutting down. She said that she had talked to his father and mother about me doing some healing with him as well while I was there. They were both open to it, and I believe they would try anything to help their son.

I arrived at the hospital and found Dominick. Melissa, his father, Devin, and his mother, Nikki, were all there. They had to keep the lights dim. He couldn't have any screen time or do anything but rest. Dominick is a sweet young man. I think he felt awkward but allowed me to put my hands on his head. I visualized reaching my energy up and seeing the white light of divine love energy flow down into me and out from my hands. My hands got warm and tingled. I was hearing that he was going to be fine. I relayed that to Dominick and his family. I held my hands on his head until I felt the tingling subside. I felt good about the energy that Dominick received.

Melissa then thanked me and took me to meet Darek, her friend. Once I saw him, I knew that I had met him before a long time ago when I was out dancing. He recognized me right away and smiled. He started to tell me a little about his son. Brayson was in another child's room. His mom went to get him and brought him out to meet me. I was immediately struck by how handsome this little guy was even with no hair and a scar across the top of his head. His eyes were so bright.

His dad introduced me to him and told him who I was, then we went into his hospital room. He decided he didn't want his parents in the room with him. We went and sat on his bed. I, as a mom, couldn't imagine what his parents were going through. Brayson wasn't able to eat due to the chemotherapy. He had no appetite and was losing weight. He was nauseous and everyone was concerned about him losing so much weight and having to maybe put him on a feeding tube.

Honestly, when I first met Brayson, I wasn't sure he was going to survive. I did feel that it would be up to him to decide. I said, "Brayson, the angels are going to work with us to help you get better. But we need to know, are you trying to go to heaven?"

He said, "No," as he shook his head.

"They are telling me you can get all better. That you are strong enough to beat this if you want to. If you decide to beat it, you will become someone who helps other people. You will inspire other people." Then I explained that angel energy comes through me and into him to help him heal.

I asked if I could put my hands on his head, and he nodded yes. I went behind him and connected. I visualized reaching up and seeing the energy come down through me and out of my hands. I put my hands on his head and the intensity of the energy made my hands all pins and needles and hot. I felt like I had just placed my hands on a hot pan. I felt this wonderful unconditional love all around us. As the energy was flowing, we talked about energy centers in the body and did a meditation visualizing colors to help open and energize his chakra centers.

I said, "Brayson, the angels are going to help you. If you need them—if something hurts or you're scared—you can ask for the angels to help. If you take three deep breaths and visualize white light around you, it will help you."

He looked tired so I left him. He thanked me, and I told him that if he ever needed me, I would come see him.

The next day, I went to the hospital to see him. His mom, Jennie, told me that he had listened to what I had said about the three breaths and the white light because he had said it during a treatment. She said that he had said, "Three deep breaths and the white light," over and over. I was glad that he was doing it and believed that it would help.

I walked into his room. The light was dim, and he had visitors. He smiled and said, "That's my calming lady." Everyone left the room. He said, "Melissa, you made me feel better, and I got a good night's sleep after you did healing on me."

I loved that. I felt such a bond with him from the first visit. He was so good about it all. I put my hands on his head, and again, felt the intense energy. We did another meditation to help with his chakra centers, then I moved around to the front to focus some healing on his stomach. He was a little nervous about me touching his belly, so I just held my hand over the stomach area. I could see him relaxing.

His mom saw how he took to me and asked me to try to get him to eat. I asked if he would try for me, and he said he would. They went and got some ice cream. I tried to feed it to him, but all he could manage was one little bite. He looked at me and said, "I'm sorry, Melissa. I just can't." I could tell that he really felt bad that he couldn't eat and didn't want to disappoint me. He was tired, so I didn't stay long. I again told him that I would be here if he needed me.

The next time I went to see him was at the end of December. I brought him healing stones in all the chakra colors. We talked about each one and how the energy of the stones can help him to heal. This time as I worked on him, I was sure that he was going to beat this. I told his mother when we were done, and we hugged. I was happy to help her to have hope. Again, I felt so horrible for what she was going through. I felt like I was helping Brayson and continued to pray for his parents.

The next time I went in, it was January. Brayson and I were talking, and I could really see and feel a difference in his energy. He was more talkative and active. As I worked on him, I felt that they were going to get good news soon. I told his mom what I was getting. She said, "I hope so." It was still scary because of the weight loss. But I actually felt excited when I had this thought.

I didn't see him for a couple of treatments because I was sick with the flu and then another sinus infection. I messaged his mother, and we both decided that we shouldn't risk exposing him to any sickness due to his low platelet count. But Jennie did message saying they did get good news— Brayson's MRI scans were clear that last Friday!

I finally saw him at the end of February. I was excited to see him. He greeted me with a hug. His eyes were bright and smiling. You wouldn't know he was sick other than the fact that he was bald and looked skinny. He never complained. I never heard him complain the entire time I worked with him. It amazed me that this boy about to turn 10 handled having a brain tumor and chemo better than I'm sure any adult would. He truly was an inspiration. As I worked on him, the now-familiar burning in my hands continued as the energy flowed. I felt so good about everything with him. Even though he still wasn't eating much, at that point, I couldn't have been convinced of anything other than his full recovery.

I went to see him at the end of March. I had missed him being at the hospital in the beginning because I was in Florida with some friends. He greeted me with a smile. He truly did seem happy to see me. He gave me a wooden car that he had decorated himself with stickers and a patch. He had written his name and the date on it. It holds a special place on my mantle in my living room.

After his healing treatment, I sat in a chair near the bed and talked with his mother. He put one of my hands on the side of his face and held my other hand in his and promptly fell asleep with my hand supporting his head. This kid owned my heart. While he was sleeping Jennie filled me in on his story, her words follow:

"Last spring, Brayson started randomly throwing up in the mornings. I thought it was anxiety driven. I took him to the ER for them to tell me that he was backed up. Then I took him to his PCP for them to tell me that he had abdominal migraines. I was accepting of the 'diagnosis' since my daughter has migraines and some of my family had them as kids as well. However, the more I thought about it, I asked for them to rule everything else out first.

"I didn't hear back, so I called—nothing. I called again—still nothing. I ended up calling and yelling, crying, and swearing, and still nothing. I ended up having to call the three specialists I wanted to get involved and explain what was happening, and they just went ahead and scheduled the appointments that I knew Brayson needed. The GI ordered labs, a liver x-ray, and a barium swallow—all of which came back fine. The allergist did a scratch test although he knew it wouldn't be related, as the vomiting always happened on an empty stomach. However, after we did the scratch test, we learned that Brayson needed an EpiPen for carrots!

"Lastly was the neurologist. She did an evaluation that was sound but still ordered an MRI to rule out brain lesions. On July 23, Brayson and I headed to Bangor for his MRI. We had big plans to go get Legos as a treat if he stayed still. Little did I know that I would be pulled into a room and told that Eastern Maine ER was expecting us—they saw something they didn't like on the MRI. I drove over to Eastern Maine Medical Center from Union Street in complete shock, having no clue what they had seen.

"We got to the ER, and once we were put in a room, I was taken down two long hallways and brought into another triage room where a stranger told me that my baby had a large mass in his left frontal lobe. From there, he was admitted to the ICU. The next day, my birthday, we were flown by life flight to Boston Children's where more pictures were taken and a plan for brain surgery was made. He was scheduled for the resection on August 1. They told us that we could leave the hospital and come back on the day of surgery, but I said that there was no way I was leaving while knowing my baby had a brain tumor.

"Days passed and things went well, all things considered. July 30 came and everything seemed fine. But in the afternoon, Brayson started complaining of some pressure. I called the nurse in because with the pressure came some different things that made me realize that he wasn't acting like himself. She suggested we wait before calling his neuro team, but I shouted at her, telling her that we weren't waiting. This wasn't my son's normal behavior.

"Before I knew it, neuro and critical response was there, and we were rushed to the MRI. The images showed hydrocephalus. He was then rushed to ICU where they pumped him full of everything they could think of to stop the pressure while they waited for the OR to be prepped. They ended up intubating him to see if rapid breathing would help release the pressure. After intubation, he was wheeled to the OR, where—THANK GOD—his brain surgeon and neuro team were able to completely remove the tumor!

"After another 10 days in the hospital, we were sent home! From there, he had his port placed and a spinal tap. In September, his six weeks of radiation started. At the end of radiation, he was given 28 days off, before his six rounds of chemo started! Each round of chemo entails three overnights at EMMC followed by 28 days off before the next round!"

On April 23, Brayson began his sixth and last round of chemotherapy. Jennie messaged me and let me know that they were in the hospital for his last round. I messaged back and said, "Does he want to see me?"

She messaged and said, "We both do!!"

I felt grateful. I really loved Brayson and was thankful for his mom allowing me this time with him. I felt like she and I really connected through this, which was another blessing. We agreed on a time and I went.

Brayson was doing so well. We did the healing session, and we talked about how he needs to stay in touch. Then I asked him if I could write this story. I told him how I thought maybe it would help other people.

He said, "Yes, but change my name." His mother agreed to me writing a story and sent me her story. I saw on Facebook how he left the hospital on the final day with a big celebration.

Brayson kicked cancer's butt! He stayed strong through it all. He is an inspiration. Not only was he strong enough to beat cancer, he never stopped caring about others more than himself. He never complained. He always radiated love. He is very special and anyone lucky enough to know him would feel that love from him. I consider myself blessed to have been a part of his life, even during this time. He will never be far from my heart and always in my prayers.

They did another MRI on May 22, 2019 after the last treatment, and Brayson's mom messaged me saying that the MRI was clear, and he was cancer-free and healing well.

Louie

March 2011

I drove from Bangor to Newington, Connecticut for training for my full-time job. On the way there, I felt that it would be a great night to write. I was away from the typical distractions and would be able to just focus on my last few stories for this book. During my drive, I had the music cranked, and the sun was shining in and my mood lifted. I had seen several numerical signs letting me know that I was on the right path right at the moment. Even when I was checking in, there was a key in the slot under the glass where someone had returned a key and it was room number 111—that will make more sense after you read a bit further.

Louie and I met a little over eight years ago. I was with a mutual friend and went to a party at his house. The moment I met him, I felt drawn to him. I initially thought that it was just because he was a handsome guy. He was behind his bar in the lounge he had built on to his house. I can remember everything about that moment even now, which is strange since I really don't have a great memory (or so my daughters tell me). What he was wearing and his smile down to every detail I can recall right now.

I was with a bunch of friends and we had all driven to Millinocket, which is about an hour north of Bangor, where I live. We had already had a few drinks at the hotel before we arrived at the party and were ready to go dancing. We first met Katie upon arriving at Louie's house. I liked her immediately, and she seemed to enjoy our loud crowd—now I'm sure she did.

We went back to the lounge area where we met Louie and drinks were offered. I knew I couldn't drink any more without having some food first. Katie pointed out that there were snacks in the kitchen, and I made my way there. I started snacking, trying to fill my belly so I'd be less tipsy. Louie came into the kitchen, and we chatted while I stuffed my face. I could tell he was just a genuinely nice guy.

Not long after, we went to the local bar where our friend was DJ-ing. We danced and laughed and had a great time with new and old friends. At one point, Louie came to dance with me. There was a magnetic energy between us. It was new yet somehow familiar; it was exciting yet comfortable. We all ended up dancing until the lights came on and it was time to go. We all decided to eat breakfast in the restaurant below the bar.

I sat with Katie, Louie, and Justin. Justin and I had had a few dates months before but remained good friends, and he started telling Katie and Louie about how we'd gone to a haunted house in Bangor. He was a realtor, and there was a gorgeous house that wasn't selling. As he took me through the house, I sensed a lot going on. We went through the house together, shutting off lights behind us as we went through the rooms. We got out to the driveway and Justin looked up, and there was a light on in one of the upstairs rooms. We were both sure that he had turned it off. He didn't take long, running in, shutting it off, and being back in the car within a moment's time.

As he was telling the story, I spoke up and said, "I'm a medium."

Louie looked at me, surprised, and said, "What?"

I said, "I'm a medium. I talk to dead people." I grinned.

He grinned and said, "Huh," like it was very interesting. And that's where it began.

A long time later, he told me that two weeks before I walked into his house that night, he had looked up at a star-filled night sky and asked for someone spiritual to come into his life. He said that many months before, he had found himself on a new spiritual journey that he was struggling to understand at times and was looking for answers.

We all started spending a lot of time together. Either a crowd of us went to Millinocket or Katie and Louie came down to Bangor.

During the summer, I spent a lot of time up there. I loved their son, Jack, who was only 4 at the time. My girls were grown and it was nice being around a small child. I love kids.

One day, Katie and I were hanging out by their pool with Jack while Louie was puttering around somewhere. I was lying on a towel near the pool. Jack and I had just been swimming. He spread out his towel right beside mine and kept inching over until he was right against me. I grinned and said, "Jack, do you need more space, or do you just want to be close to me?"

He said, "I just want to be close to you." Then he said, "Melissa, if you need anything to eat or drink, just tell me and I'll tell my mom to get it for you." So sweet, I loved him.

Louie and I had many conversations about our beliefs. He was and still is the guy who wants to figure out the science behind all of this. And I was fascinated listening to him describe the hows and whys of the universe. He shared some of his experiences. He knew things were going to happen as a kid and described seeing spirits. I think that, because of those experiences, he needed answers.

We started taking a mediumship development class on Monday nights from an amazing teacher named Patty Palmer, a Reverend at church. I was experiencing more during these classes with Louie's energy beside me than I had before. I started to be able to do trance mediumship. I could feel energies take over my body and speak through me. I was aware but felt pushed to the side as I allowed this to happen. The first time it happened, I felt like I was rising out of my chair, and it startled me, so I quickly grabbed onto Louie and it stopped. I think that, after that, it happened much more slowly and gently. As time went on, Louie began to trance as well; he would not remember any of it because he would be so deep. When he went into trance, I felt like I was in a suspended state, feeling my energy go to him. It drained him, and he would often have a bad headache from doing it.

We took many classes during the summers at the spiritualist camps. We had at least three different mediums tell us that we are each other's battery when doing spirit work and that we work well together because of our similar energy. I have described it as if Louie and I are the only ones of the same type of aliens on a strange planet. I feel as if we are a part of the same something. Whether we refer to it as soul mates or soul twins, I have a connection with him like no other. We can get very busy and caught up in our lives and not see each other for months but then share similar dreams with each other that occurred on the same night. Very frequently our texts to each must pass in the air because just as I hit send, I receive a text from him. We often text on 11:11 and 1:11—we both believe that those numbers are indicators that we are on our right path.

I have seen several past lives of ours. One time, we did a past-life meditation CD together, listening to it through headphones. It was so detailed and real while I was in it. I saw a life that was back in really early times. I'm guessing 1600 maybe. I was wearing a cloak and we were meeting in the forest. We were running away to be together. For some reason, we were not allowed to be together and running away was the only answer. It was a cold evening, and the vision was so real as we ran through the woods. The next scene was us waking up to men around us. They grabbed me from Louie and held me while they beat him to death. I watched, screaming in horror. They brought me back to the village and put me in a rack. Hands and head stuck through the holes, I was stoned and had garbage thrown at me. I felt like it didn't matter—I wanted to die and be with Louie. Then the vision was over. There were two more that I saw with as much detail, and one or the other of us always died, and we were never together.

When the meditation CD was done, I was so excited to see if Louie had experienced the same thing or if he'd been shown other past lives. He opened his eyes and looked at me and blinked a few times.

I said, "That was awesome! What did you see?"

He grinned sheepishly and said, "Nothing, I fell asleep."

I was disappointed but laughingly gave him a hard time. Then I told him every detail of what I had experienced.

One night, we did a past life regression for him with me guiding the direction. It was very interesting—I was recording it, and it looked like it was recording, but when we were done, it had only recorded a few seconds. Under hypnosis, Louie talked about Natives being around him. He was trying to get away and felt an arrow pierce into his back. I continued to ask questions.

He said, "I'm dead." Then he was silent, but I could tell he was still seeing something.

I said, "Where are you now?"

He said, "Outside the window, looking in." He described seeing his sister and his father grieving over his death. Then he said, "You are my sister." Then he went into the white light and was greeted by an angel—it was very powerful for him. The messages he received from the angel were in part about being in front of audiences and choices he would have in his future. When I brought him out of hypnosis, his eyes were watery, and he looked at me and said, "What did you do to me?"

That was one of the first times we received messages about being on stage together. Bonnie Lee gave me messages about the events we now do together years before they came to fruition.

We created these events that I called "Power in Belief." It was channeled; I really cannot take credit. I talk about my experiences, Louie does a talk about energy and the science behind how what we do is possible. He is still kind of in the closet about being a medium though. We have other people come and share their healing techniques, akashic record experience, and life experiences, and we do gallery style readings. It is an empowering, uplifting day for all. We love doing them and the feedback that we get feels great. I believe we met and were meant to do these types of events to raise awareness, to restore faith, and to make people realize that they are never alone and they control their happiness.

A few years ago, I realized another interesting coincidence/synchronicity… well, I don't believe in coincidence after all I have experienced. The day my liver failed and I was supposed to have died was the same exact date he and Katie were married. I believe this is his path and I was supposed to stay here to help him on it. Was that part of the divine plan to keep me here so I could be his battery and push him into this life of teaching? Someday, we will have the answers. I do know that I would not be as far as I am without his love and support. To have someone experience the weird things that you do in a similar—if not exact same—way, is so validating. If we are crazy, at least we are in it together.

Louie's family is wonderful. I loved them all upon our first meeting. I met his mom and dad at his camp along with Darcy, his sister, and her three daughters. I cannot describe enough how connected I feel to his family even though I haven't spent a lot of time with them. I told Darcy once that if I kept my eyes closed, I would swear it was Louie standing by me—her energy is just a beautiful as his.

The first time I met Darcy and her daughters, Molly, Eva, and Lila, was at their family camp in Millinocket. Darcy was telling me how she was worried about Eva and how she would see things. She was almost 5 years old if I'm remembering correctly and was so shy around new people.

She said, "Melissa, she has a hard time going into the camp because of the people, but it is all family."

I looked at Eva and felt for her. I remember that feeling of being pained to talk to people. I said, "Darcy, I think she is overwhelmed by the energy. I could do some healing work on her, if that is okay, to see if we can seal out the energy so she isn't so sensitive." I was "getting" to create a stronger aura; I needed to channel energy into her.

About a minute later, while Darcy and I were still talking, Eva climbed the stairs and sat so close to me that we were practically touching. Darcy's jaw dropped open and her eyes got huge in shock as she mouthed, "I cannot believe that just happened." I talked to Eva and put my hands on her. I felt the energy flow. We really connected. She and I have a bond even now even though I don't think she remembers that moment.

Years later, I had an experience that I will never forget that Louie and I shared. It was late on a Sunday night and I was taking an online course. My computer kept freezing up, and I was very frustrated. It was an eight-hour course, and I just wanted to be done already. The later it got, the more frustrated I became. I had to work the next day.

Out of the corner of my eye, I saw a shadow go by. I knew it was a spirit, and I don't usually see them that way, so it made me pause and do a "gut" check. That is how I know whether it is something good or not so nice. I felt fine, so I said out loud, "Whoever you are, I need to get this done. I don't have time right now." A few minutes later, I saw it go by me again. I did another gut check and said, "You are welcome, I'm just busy."

Not long after, I finally finished. It was after 11 p.m. if I am remembering correctly. I was getting ready for bed and felt this push to look at my phone, which had been on silent. I picked it up and there were multiple messages from Louie, Katie, and Jacob, our close friend. I read Louie's first: "My dad just passed."

First there was intense shock. Then, immediately, there was Louie's dad, Carl's, spirit right in my face. He said, *I knew they were going to be okay. The door to paradise opened, and I went through. If you knew everyone was going to be okay, wouldn't you go too?*

I knew I would. Then I had this vision of a black room with a white light door and a shadow of a man going through it. As sad as I was for Louie and his family, I felt great for Carl. I immediately messaged Louie and tried to comfort him and said if he needed me I'd drive up tonight. He said that wasn't necessary and we would talk the next day.

The next morning, I looked for something inspiring and comforting to send to Louie. I came across this inspirational quote on a picture just like my vision. It was a black room with a door of white light with the shadow of a man going through it. I cropped off the saying and sent it to Louie with the words his dad had told me the night before and said, "Your dad showed me this last night."

Louie wrote back and said that was very validating for him, and that he would explain when he saw me. Katie messaged me and asked me to come up the next day to be with Louie. We sat and talked, and he told me that the night his dad passed, he was just falling asleep and he saw a shadow go by the end of his bed. At that point, I hadn't told him that I had seen his dad as a shadow twice before I knew Carl had passed. He continued, "I knew it was Dad. Then I had a vision exactly like the picture you sent with the door of white light and Dad's shadow going through it."

It was amazing how Carl had shown us the exact same thing. I was blessed to be able to validate what Louie was saying with my own experience.

Carl has come through a few times since he passed. He helped me order a memorial canvas of a picture of him with a wonderful inspirational quote that I gave to Louie, his mom, and Darcy. I was able to give messages to Louie's mom, Barbara, one evening last summer at their camp. More recently, in March of this year when I was on vacation in Florida, I was visiting some friends who live a few hours away from Darcy. I had made plans to visit both of them after helping my friend Matt drive down because he was moving there.

I woke up at my friend Mike and Steph's house alone—they had both gone to work. I was excited by the idea of this book. I had tried four years ago to write a book and got to page 12 but didn't know where to go from there. The thought that popped in my head—divine guidance for sure—was that I should write a book with a bunch of short stories. Most of these stories I have told for years—this would be easy.

The next day, I rented a car and drove to Darcy's house. I should have arrived at about 12:30 p.m. but I had to stop and use the restroom so many times, and one time, the restroom was closed and I had to find another one. I was much later arriving than I thought I would be. Barbara was there visiting and knew that I was on my way. I was thinking about Louie and this book, and I happened to glance at the exit I was passing...of course, Exit 111. I smiled to myself and sent up a thanks to the universe. Then I felt Carl in the car with me. 11:11 and 1:11 were important numbers to him as well.

When I finally arrived at Darcy's house, I shut off the ignition and noticed that it was 1:11 p.m. I, again, smiled. I couldn't believe the timing! I knocked on the door, and Barbara opened it. We greeted each other, and I couldn't wait to tell her. I said before I was even in the door, "Guess what time it was when I shut off the ignition to the car?"

She smiled, knowing my answer before I said it. "Melissa it's a God Wink." I hadn't heard of that before. She explained as she went to pick up the book from where she left it, "It's a book that is a series of short stories that are all about things that happen beyond coincidence. I went and picked it up at the library yesterday."

Another sign I'm on track with my short stories, I thought. I had a wonderful time with Barbara over the two days I was there. I felt really close to her by the time I left. Darcy, Robert, and the girls could not have made me feel more loved and welcomed. I was sad that I had planned such a short trip. I love that family! I had to leave at 4 a.m. on Saturday morning. Darcy and Eva got up to see me off. I hugged them tightly and thanked them. I cannot wait until they all come to Maine this summer.

Meanwhile, Louie and I are still doing our thing. I am trying to convince him that once this book is published, we need to hit the road and do our events in places other than just Maine. He always looks skeptical, but I truly believe it is on our path and that you will see us doing what we love to do. I have threatened that I am ready to fly—he can come with, or I'm going without him.

We will see what happens. To be continued…

About the Author

Melissa Gabriel lives in Bangor, Maine and is a professional psychic/medium and spiritual healer. She has been using her abilities of clairvoyance (seeing), clairaudience (hearing), and clairsentience (feeling) to help guide others for over 18 years. Through private or group readings, she has assisted in connecting people with their spirit relatives, guides, and angels. She is also a certified hypnotherapist, specializing in past-life regression.

Melissa is president on the board of the Harrison D. Barrett Spiritualist Church in Bangor, Maine. She serves spiritualist churches and camps as an inspirational speaker, teacher, and guest medium and has been teaching mediumship development classes for eight years.

Melissa organizes spiritual and inspirational events that teach people the spiritual and scientific ways they can find their inner peace and happiness.

You can find her Facebook page at **https://www.facebook.com/angel connection11** and her YouTube channel at **https://bit.ly/2pTnxtw**.